SO-ABN-967

The Down Under Cookbook

THE
DOWN UNDER
COOKBOOK

An Authentic Guide to Australian
Cooking and Eating Traditions

Graeme Newman

Harrow and Heston
New York

Copyright ©1987, Graeme Newman.

All rights reserved. No part of this book may be reproduced
or transmitted in any form or by any means, electronic or
mechanical, including photocopying, recording, or by any
information storage and retrieval system, without permission
in writing from the publisher.

The author and publishers are grateful to Keith McKenry
and *Bunyip Bush Enterprises* for permission to reproduce *At
The Sign Of The Ravenous Goanna*, taken from *The Spirit of
the People: Modern Australian Recitations*, 1983.

Harrow and Heston, Publishers,
Stuyvesant Plaza,
P.O. Box 3934,
Albany, New York, 12203

Library of Congress Catalog Card Number: 87-80068

ISBN: 0-911577-11-4

Printing number
9 8 7 6 5 4 3 2 1

Cover: The Domes of Mount Olga, compliments of the
Australian Tourist Commission.

Consulting Editor: Joan Newman
Art Work: Amanda, Clancy, and Tamsin Newman

Contents

Dedicated To Mums Everywhere
Who Have Given The Best
Parts Of Their Lives
To the Kitchen

At The Sign Of The Ravenous Goanna

At the sign of the Ravenous Goanna
I went to have a feed:
The thought was so exquisite
I was trembling at the knees.

They have Lamingtons in Batter,
  And Licorice All-sorts Pie,
And Lamb's Fry served in Cold Custard
  That you just *have* to try.

Vegemite, and Lipton's Tea
  Dished up with Rabbit Stew,
And Two Fruits, lovely Two Fruits,
  To thrill you through and through.

Tomato Sauce and Chocolate Frogs,
  And Saunder's Malt Extract
(Just pity all the poor lost souls
  Who've never tasted that!)

Dims Sims, Chooks, and Chico Rolls,
  And good old boiled Galah;
Floaters and Vick's Vapo-Rub
  For old men with catarrh.

Polly Waffles, Prickly Pear,
  Johnny Cakes and Billy Tea;
Stewed Prune and Baked Bean Jaffles
  —Oh, Australian food for me!

There's Scotty's Wild Stuff Stew of course,
  And Oysters from the Rocks,
And Wine, the nectar of the Grape,
  Served from a cardboard box.

Peck's Fish Paste and Passion Fruit;
  Teddy Bears with Robur Tea;
Pavlova, Chips and Choo-Choo Bars
  —The Height of Luxury!

Yabbies, Jaffas, Saveloys,
  Damper, Crays, Nardoo;
Jumbuk Paté for the pseudes,
  Butter Menthols for the 'flu.

There's a dish for every taste and mood,
  And they sing Australian songs.
So come to the Ravenous Goanna, friends,
  And bring *your* friends along.

—Keith McKenry, 1970s.

1

The Australian Melting Pot

$\boxed{\text{T}}$he winds of a million years have made Australia into what she is today. There are no jagged peaks in the Outback. Instead, there are rocky outcrops worn round and smooth by the endless grinding of the elements. The reds of the Australian center are matched in tone and intensity only by the scorched surface of Mars. It is a Timeless Land, as the great Australian novelist Eleanor Dark observed many years ago.

The Australian Aborigines are Australia's timeless people, the original Australians. There are many aboriginal folk stories that preserve a sense of the sheer age of the land and her people, often referred to as the "dream time" (see *dream cake*, page 122). Australia's unusual animals loom large in these stories, and well they should.

Australia boasts animal species that are unique: Furred animals that lay eggs (the platypus); others that suckle their young in pouches (kangaroos); still others that get high on a naturally found drug (koalas); birds whose calls sound as raucous laughter (kookaburra); yet other birds that mimic all the sounds of the bush (the lyre bird).

Into this giant landscape stepped the English, in the 1770s searching for somewhere to dump their convicts. The American Revolution made it impossible for the English to use America as its prison. There are many theories as to how the Australian national character—carefree (epitomized by the com-

mon saying, "She'll be right mate"), a bit abrasive and a most
disarming, earthy, sense of humor—has evolved from that of
criminals. Sir Robert Menzies (Australia's conservative prime
minister for some 18 years ending in 1966) was always ready
with an answer to those who made fun of Australia's convict
ancestry. In a speech at the Jefferson Oration at Charlotteville,
Virginia on the 4th of July, 1963, Sir Robert wryly noted:

> ...the records show that the great majority of per-
> sons convicted in England during the transporta-
> tion era remained in England.

The influence of the English on Australian lifestyles and
customs is vast. We have them to thank for the national sport
of cricket. Australia's unique sport, "Aussie Rules" football
was derived from Irish football. And we have the English to
thank for our Irish heritage, since a large portion of convicts
sent to Australia were Irish. Our rich array of folk songs and
poetry are directly attributable to the oppression of convicts
and settlers by the British and their lackeys in the early colonial
period.

Most of all, though, the English have influenced Australian
food, cooking and eating habits. Many, perhaps most, of the
recipes in this book bear a strong similarity to English dishes.
Fruit cake, steamed pudding, roast lamb, pasties and many
others, are directly identifiable in English cuisine. But they
have also become a central feature in Australian cuisine, and
reasonably included as "Australian."

What is an authentic Australian dish? My answer to this
difficult question is, any dish that Australians have taken to
call their own. A dish that they eat as part of everyday life.
Fish and Chips are English. But they are Australian too, and
Australians have given them their special Australian "character," if one can refer to a French fry as having character. (Does
one ever hear the claim that the English chip is really French?)

The Timeless Land is not timeless when it comes to eating. The eating habits of Australians have changed, and are
changing rapidly. This is because of Australia's melting pot.

The Australian continent is about the same size as the continental United States, yet its population is only 15 million.

Her scarce resource is people, and successive governments have responded to this scarcity by well orchestrated immigration programs. Today, there is a tremendous variety of peoples living in Australia's cities. In fact, Melbourne (capital of the State of Victoria) is the third largest Greek speaking city in the world. The influence on Australia's restaurants, therefore, by peoples from the Mediterranean, and more recently from parts of the Pacific Islands and South East Asia, is considerable. It is only a matter of time until the cooking traditions of these countries seep into the traditional Australian kitchens.

Before that happens, if it has not already happened, it is my hope that this book will at least record, and at most preserve, some of the special Australian cooking traditions that I remember from my childhood, and that still continue in traditional pockets of Australian town and suburban life . Many of the recipes in this book have been taken from my mother's old handwritten cookbook, along with a motley collection of recipes written on scraps of paper, no doubt by her many visitors with whom she drank countless cups of tea. Many other friends and relatives have kindly provided me with their favorites.

There are a few small problems with these recipes, which I have tried to overcome. My mother cooked most of her life on a wood burning stove and oven. Her recipes mostly said, "warm," "moderate," or "hot" oven—not very precise. The way she established whether the oven was ready, was to open the door and put her hand in. It has been a bit of a challenge to translate these imprecise measurements into temperature readings.

The quantities are also difficult to translate, as Australian measurements, especially tablespoons, dessertspoons and liquid measures are quite different from the American. I have developed over the years a way to convert these measures, so that the quantities in the recipes should be accurate. Nevertheless, I would suggest, just in case I have messed up here or there, that you treat the measurements as guides to be adjusted if you think things are not going quite right.

About the Australian Outback, and bush cooking: Four-fifths of Australia's 15 million population live in its 5 largest cities. This makes Australia one of the most sparsely populated yet most urbanized countries of the world! Many Australians have probably never seen a kangaroo in the wild (though if you know where to go, this is quite a simple thing to do), let alone actually try to live in the Outback. When I was a boy, I was fortunate enough to camp out often in the bush, largely as a Boy Scout. (The funny thing was that all the books were English, including the star constellations of the Northern Hemisphere!) I learned a lot of very useful skills, and my wife and I have enjoyed passing these things on to our kids when we have camped throughout America. Most of the dishes one can cook in America, although a few of the ingredients aren't available in the American forest, such as Tiger Snake.

About the Australian language ("strine"): Americans frequently ask me whether Australians speak English. I usually grin in reply and say, "More or less." Of course, we do speak English, but with a heavy accent, and the voice directed somewhere down one's chest. If you say "newspiper" instead of "newspaper" you will have closely reproduced the typical Australian vowel sound. However, it is not so much the accents that make Australians difficult to understand, but the many unique expressions. There is a whole vocabulary, along with unusual usage of common words that can make conversation with an Australian something of an experience. An American friend of mine once gave a speech to a large audience of Australian police, urging that people get off their fannies and work for a particular project. He was unaware that "fanny" does not mean "backside" in Australia, but rather refers to a very private female part!

Throughout the book I have included notations on Australian language, without which it would be difficult to describe eating and cooking traditions. Accordingly, I could say, "bon appétit" but the Australian saying is more earthy, in keeping with our convict ancestry:

> Two, Four, Six, Eight,
> Bog in, don't wait!

...and enjoy your tucker (food)!

2

Pie 'n Sauce

...and other Dinkum Aussie Foods

To be "fair dinkum" in the Australian language is to be "true blue." None the wiser? Both expressions mean absolutely pure and authentic. And that's what these foods are. They're pure Australian. It doesn't matter that they may have existed somewhere else (in Once-Great Britain, for example) long before they became part of every Australian's life. What is important is that they *are now* totally unique to Australia. A spectator sport would be unthinkable without them. Just as a baseball game would be unthinkable without hot dogs.

Should you go to the cricket or footy (an Australian Rules football game) you will have many chances to buy a pie and sauce (and, if you're that way inclined, a can of Fosters beer to go with it). Meat pies are *the* take out food in Australia. Some tasteless people, certainly not dinkum Aussies, have described Aussie meat pies as gravy encased in pieces of cardboard pastry. This may (only *may*) be true for mass produced pies, but it certainly is not true for those made at home.

MAISIE'S PASTIES†

Along with fish and chips, hot dogs and pies, pasties are a favorite take-out food in Australia. Their aroma while cooking is nothing short of tantalizing. The unusual blend of vegetables and meat, encased in a delicious pastry makes them unique as take out food—and probably the most nutritious.

I had two uncles who were pastrycooks (bakers) and my mother was an accomplished cook as well. They all made terrific pasties. Of all my childhood memories, those of taste stand out, and those of eating pasties (and sniffing them while cooking) are by far and away the most prominent. It took a long time to get this recipe into some form that was dependable, as my mother did not use exact measurements for many of her favorites. One simply sifted some flour and margarine, mixed up the vegetables, and there it was. The oven temperature was also difficult to establish, because, as I mentioned earlier, she cooked for most of her life in a wood oven, with her hand as the oven thermometer. However, I have cooked pasties in America many times, and will vouch for this recipe.

I have found, much to my disappointment, that some Americans do not like pasties, and my kids certainly are not too thrilled about them. This seems to be because of the turnip or rutabagas, which are not common vegetables. One could make them without these vegetables, but then the pasties would lose their distinctive taste. I have not yet relented. When I cook pasties all vegetables are included, and if the kids won't eat them, well...all the more for me. Pasties are eaten with plenty of ketchup (tomato sauce to Australians). I like them made with lots of pepper.

---

†Pronounced *pah-stees*, probably of Cornish origin, but definitely now Australian through and through. They are sometimes a different shape to that described in this recipe, which is the typical Cornish pasty shape.

MAISIE'S PASTIES

(CONTINUED)

FILLING

1	pound lean ground beef	1	pound potatoes
1	carrot	1	small turnip or
2-3	onions		rutabagas
	salt and pepper		

Chop finely or mince all vegetables and add to meat. Mix thoroughly, add salt and pepper.

PASTRY

2	cups self rising flour	$\frac{1}{2}$	pound margarine
$\frac{1}{3}$	cup water	1	pinch salt

Sift flour and salt, rub in margarine until mixture looks like bread crumbs. Mix in water gradually, stirring with a wooden spoon until dough makes a stiff ball. If in doubt, it is better that the dough is a little moist than dry. Turn on to floured board and knead lightly. Cut into 12 pieces and knead into rounds. Roll out each round as thin as possible so that dough may be lifted and shaped without breaking. Spoon mixture into center of each piece of dough, then with wet finger moisten the edges of each dough round. Lift pastry up from sides, bringing into the center, and pinch together all across the top. Begin at center and work towards the outside†. Place pasties on greased cookie tray. Paint with egg or milk, then prick tops with fork. Bake for $\frac{1}{2}$ to $\frac{3}{4}$ hour at 350^0-400^0.

---

†See page 10. Instead of pinching together at the top, sometimes the mixture is place on one side of the round, and the other half folded all the way over and pinched around the edge, making a kind of half circle shape (something like an apple turnover). Puff pastry is also sometimes used.

PIE AND SAUCE

Here is my favorite recipe. It is for a 9 inch pie pan. The pies one may buy in the store are usually a small one-serving size. The traditional shape was an oval, but this tradition disappeared many years ago, no doubt because the shape could not be adapted easily to mass production. Bought pies also have a pie crust on top and bottom, otherwise they would be difficult to eat in the hands. Even so, they are real hard to bite into without gravy shooting out over your shirt.

1	tablespoon butter	2	tablespoons onion
$\frac{1}{4}$	cup celery		(finely chopped)
	(finely chopped)	$\frac{1}{4}$	cup carrots
$\frac{1}{2}$-$\frac{3}{4}$	pound ground beef or		(finely chopped)
	cubed steak	1	cup beef stock

Roll beef in flour, or sprinkle 1 tablespoon of flour over ground beef. Sauté beef in butter with onion, carrot and celery, until meat is brown and vegetables bright in color. Cover with beef stock, add salt and pepper to taste, and simmer covered until meat is tender. Place in greased pie pan and top with pie crust (use pastry from *Maisie's Pasties,* page 7). Bake for 10-15 minutes at 425° or until pastry is golden brown. Serve hot, always with plenty of ketchup (tomato sauce in Australian).

For *STEAK AND KIDNEY PIE*, the English ancestor of these pies, add 1 small chopped beef kidney to meat mixture.

Many variations are possible with this recipe. If you are entertaining, line muffin tins with thin pastry, fill with pie filling, and cap. These party pies are always a raving success. Try other variations: add a couple of spoonfuls of frozen peas to the mixture 5 minutes before meat is cooked. Better still, when sautéing meat and vegetables, add 1 tablespoon of red wine, preferably claret. Or, try a teaspoon of port (yes, port). Can be frozen and reheated a week or two later.

MUM'S SAUSAGE ROLLS

I have eaten these little beauties in New Zealand, Scotland
England, Canada and even in Delaware, U.S.A. They never
taste the same as the real Australian, home made sausage roll,
especially the ones my mother used to make. The difference is
in the pastry.

1   yolk of egg $\frac{1}{2}$ pound sausage meat
$\frac{1}{2}$ pound pastry

Crust: Use pastry from *Maisie's Pasties,* page 7. Roll out
into oblong shape and cut into 8 even pieces by cutting first
straight down the center of pastry, then across 3 times. Divide
sausage meat into 8 pieces, roll each piece into a sausage shape
and sprinkle all over with flour. Place each sausage on pastry,
moisten edges of pastry with water. Fold over pastry so that
it covers sausage and meets on other side (see page 10). Press
together with back of a flat knife. Beat yolk of egg and brush
on rolls. Bake in hot oven (375⁰-400⁰) for 20-30 minutes.

SECRET: Make sure your pastry is not too short (too dry),
or it will be difficult to work over sausage, and will also crumble
when your eager guests try to get their mouths around these
delicious morsels. There is a problem with the sausage meat.
In Australia this meat is usually finely ground beef, but sometimes pork is used. I have tried pork sausage here, which is
fine, but be sure you buy extra lean, otherwise you may end up
with sausage rolls floating around in a sea of fat. Ideally, the
sausage should be finely ground as in pork sausage, but shaped
lean ground beef, while not perfect, still provides a delicious
roll. Link sausages are also O.K.

When you are accomplished at rolling the dough very thin,
little party sausage rolls are a popular item. They are also
wonderful cold—perfect for a midnight snack.

Sausage rolls are always eaten with plenty of ketchup.

PORK PIES

4	ounces pork	$\frac{1}{2}$	apple
$\frac{1}{2}$	onion	2	tablespoons flour
	salt and pepper	$\frac{1}{2}$	pound pastry
$\frac{1}{2}$	cup water		

Mince the pork, or ask your butcher to do it for you. Chop apple and onion very fine, add flour, salt and pepper and water, mixing well. Simmer until apple and onion are soft. For pie crust, use pastry from *Maisie's Pasties*, page 7. Line well greased muffin pans with thin pie crust. Fill with mixture and cover with pastry. Paint tops with milk, and prick with fork. Bake in oven 375^0-400^0 for $\frac{1}{2}$ an hour.

Pork pies are definitely not a part of Australian cooking any more. They are certainly still very much a part of the English scene. One can find them along with scotch eggs in just about every English pub. Not so in Australia. Old Australians consider pork to be very "sickly" only to be eaten on very special occasions. In fact, Australian pork does tend to be less lean than American. But, in deference to our wonderful English heritage, I include this recipe for pork pies. Actually, they're delicious. They probably were edged out of Australian pubs by beef pies and pasties which do go better with beer. Pork pies taste better with apple cider (effervescent and alcoholic, of course).

Pasty   *Sausage Roll*

EGG AND BACON PIE

The chances are that, just as in the United States, real Australian men don't eat quiche, but you can be sure that they *do* eat egg and bacon pie which is very similar, if not better than quiche. Try it, and decide for yourself.

4	large eggs	$\frac{1}{2}$	cup milk
2	tablespoons parsley, chopped	1	small onion (finely chopped)
$\frac{1}{4}$	cup grated cheese	$\frac{1}{2}$	cup chopped bacon
8	ounces pastry		

For pie crust use pastry from *Maisie's Pasties*, page 7. Roll out pastry thin and line a 9 inch pie pan. Place eggs, cheese, onions, milk and salt and pepper in pan and beat with a fork until blended well. Heat over slow flame, like cooking scrambled eggs. Stir continually. When mixture has consistency of lightly scrambled eggs mix in parsley. Pour into pie pan and cover with pieces of bacon (lean bacon is best). Bake at 350⁰ for 30 minutes. It's O.K. to eat this pie with ketchup. This is a wonderful dish to cook for house guests who don't usually eat breakfast. The aroma will reach everyone's bedroom and to their surprise they will find themselves irresistibly drawn to the brekkie (breakfast) table.

VARIATION: After pouring egg mixture into pie shell, break 4 eggs on to the top of the mixture. Cook as above.

Egg and Bacon Pie

RUPANYUP RISSOLES

These are interesting hybrids, half hamburger and half cro-
quette.

$\frac{1}{4}$	pound ground beef	$\frac{1}{2}$	teaspoon basil
4	tablespoons bread crumbs	2	tablespoons parsley (finely chopped)
1	egg	$\frac{1}{3}$	cup beef bouillon

Lightly brown ground beef over high heat. Add remaining ingredients, lower heat and stir until mixture is quite thick. Add
breadcrumbs or bouillon until correct thickness is obtained.
Remove from pan and set aside to cool.

1	egg	$\frac{1}{2}$	cup bread crumbs
4	tablespoons flour	2	tablespoons parsley
	pepper and salt		(finely chopped)

Take large tablespoons of the mixture, form into patties, and
roll in flour, salt and pepper. Beat egg and brush over rissole,
then roll on bread crumbs, pushing crumbs into surface with a
knife. Heat cooking oil, and when quite hot, place rissoles in
pan and fry each side until golden brown. When cooked, drain
on paper, serve garnished with parsley, and with brown sauce
(below). Ketchup or a packet of brown gravy is also fine.

BROWN SAUCE

1	piece carrot	1	small piece rutabagas
1	piece onion	1	small stick celery
1	tablespoon parsley	$\frac{1}{4}$	teaspoon thyme
$\frac{1}{4}$	teaspoon marjoram	2	bay leaves
4	peppercorns	$\frac{1}{2}$	ounce oil
1	slice bacon	1	small tomato
$1\frac{1}{4}$	cups bouillon	2	tablespoons flour

Next page please...

Chop vegetables. Tie up herbs in small cloth bag. Dry vegetables with paper towel. Heat oil and fry all vegetables, except tomato, until a light brown. Stir frequently. Add tomato and stir a little more. Add flour, salt to taste, pepper, and brown well. Pour in bouillon, stirring until boiling. Add herbs and bacon then simmer for $\frac{1}{2}$ hour. Strain and remove fat.

Serve separately, or pour over rissoles. Minced or chopped leftover meat may be substituted for the ground beef.

My mother made rissoles often, using minced up or diced leftover meat, whether lamb, veal or beef. In fact, this was the original ingredient for rissoles, just as leftover meat was traditionally used for that other favorite, Shepherd's Pie. I haven't included the latter in this book, because just about every American Cookbook one opens has a recipe for it. The brown gravy can also be bought in powder form in Australian shops (called *Gravox*) which makes a delicious gravy more appealing to my taste than any I have found in American stores.

Rupanyup, in whose honor these rissoles are named, is a small town in the Wimmera district of Victoria, one of Australia's smallest States (Tasmania is smaller). This is the heart of the wheat growing district, a country of wide flat plains forever golden with wheat, a rich red earth. The shrieks of cockatoos as they flock in great white clouds live in my memory, though I have visited there only once.

Cockatoos

TOAD IN THE HOLE

This meat and batter dish is popular for breakfast, lunch or dinner.

$\frac{1}{2}$ cup self rising flour   1   egg
1   ounce margarine $\frac{1}{2}$ pound sausage meat†
$\frac{3}{4}$ cup milk   salt

Sift flour, add melted margarine and stir into flour, gradually adding milk (make tepid). Beat well, fold in beaten egg just before using. Shape sausage meat into sausage shapes. Grease baking pan and place in oven until very hot (oven at 400⁰). Pour in the batter, drop in the sausages so that they lie in one direction. Bake for 35 minutes. Best served with thick brown gravy, or ketchup.

---

†You will have to experiment with sausage meat. If you decide to use pork sausage, ask your butcher (if you can find one) for pork sausage that is very lean, otherwise you may have underground rivers of fat, rather than toads in the hole. If you would rather play it safe, the older, though less common Australian version of this dish-with-the-strange-name was made with pieces of good quality steak or cubed lamb. We use extra lean ground beef.

Yes, this dish is also essentially English in origin. The Australian version is far better, though, because it uses snags (the long thin ones) as the sausage meat. Sausage links could be substituted. I used to plead with my mother to make this dish. We had fun as kids, searching for the "toads."

Platypus

3

Sandwiches and Scones

|M|y American friends who have visited Australia have been shocked at what they rather uncharitably termed "the little things Australians call sandwiches." Not only are they the wrong *size*, my friends say, but they are often the wrong color!

When my friends and relatives from Australia visit us here, they are aghast at the amount of filling and sheer size of American sandwiches. I have become accustomed to the, roughly, quarter pound of cold cuts I will get when I buy a sandwich in a typical deli in the American North East. When they see these sandwiches, my Australian relatives spend much of the rest of their visit pointing out all the fat Americans they can, and trying to order *half* a sandwich. I'd rather not take sides in the serious difference in values between our two countries, but I think I can say why there is such a difference—or at least why the Australian sandwiches are so small.

There are basically two kinds of sandwiches in Australia— those that are cut by thousands of Mums everyday for school and work lunches, and those prepared for afternoon teas. There is not a great deal of difference between the two, as far as fillings go, but they are both vastly different from an American sandwich. Here's why.

Australian sandwiches are almost always cut from a small sized sandwich loaf (the most common are white and "wholemeal" though these days there is about as big a variety as in America). Without exception, the bread for every sandwich is cut thinner than in America, in fact the thinner the better.

In addition, each slice of bread is spread with a thin layer of butter or margarine. Again, this is without exception, no matter the filling—even peanut butter. (When I make a peanut butter sandwich at home, I always put butter in it, much to the disgust of my kids. I respond by threatening to throw up when they put jelly in theirs.)

If one is preparing sandwiches for an afternoon tea or a kid's birthday party (yes, believe it or not, there are sandwiches that are quite acceptable to kids for a birthday party—read on!) the practice is to cut off all the crusts, making the overall size of the bread slice even smaller. Then the sandwiches are cut diagonally so that small dainty triangles are produced. Squares and rectangles are also acceptable, but they are the exception.

Now for the "meager fillings." It is largely because of the butter in the sandwiches that there is less filling. If one buys a roast beef sandwich in Australia one may receive two or three slices, four at the most in the sandwich. It is not quantity that is important, but a particular taste. I should add that meats tend to be much more cooked in Australia than the United States. Anyway there is little doubt in my mind that it is the acquired taste of butter in the sandwich that satisfies the Australian appetite. If there were any more filling the sandwich would be too sickly.

The more usual sandwich lunch would be "two rounds of sandwiches" (although the sandwiches are square, not round). This means 4 slices of bread made into two sandwiches, each sandwich possibly with a different filling, but a filling no more than $\frac{1}{4}$ inch thick. In a sandwich shop, packets of mixed sandwiches are common. Again, these will have very meager fillings, by American standards, but will have three or four different fillings, and will usually contain 2 rounds of sandwiches (i.e. 4 slices of bread).

Why are some Aussie sandwiches the wrong color ? See page 20...

SANDWICHES FOR SPECIAL OCCASIONS

These are always cut into dainty sizes, as described above, and served in the afternoon with a cup of tea, if for an adult occasion. The most famous is the *Vegemite Sandwich* introduced, at least in name, to curious Americans by the *Men At Work* singing group.

VEGEMITE^{TM} SANDWICH

If for special occasions, which include parties, special teas, or for someone who is feeling down (Vegemite†is the chicken soup of Australian Mums) these sandwiches are often served open style. The bread should be as fresh as possible.

Spread bread lightly with butter or margarine. Place a *small* amount of Vegemite on the tip of a knife and spread *very* thinly over bread and butter. Cut into dainty shapes. Butter and Vegemite may also be spread on any type of cracker. Be warned! I have not met many Americans who liked this stuff. It's a taste that is carefully cultivated among Australian kids virtually from birth. It also tastes very salty, although now there is a version that is salt free.

It says on the Vegemite jar label that this dark, iodine colored substance is a vegetable yeast extract. Folklore has it that many years ago, a bright young chemist developed it from the enormous amounts of byproducts from beer manufacture. Perhaps you have not heard, but Australians are devoted beer drinkers.

†Vegemite^{TM} is a trademark of Kraft Foods (believe it or not!). I have occasionally found it in gourmet food stores, although its (lesser) counterpart, Marmite (a beef extract a bit like bouillon paste) is more common (also, English and not Australian, therefore naturally of less importance). You can send away for Vegemite in the United States to: *Australasia Ventures, 3100 Airway Avenue, Suite 106, Costa Mesa, California 92626.*

HUNDREDS AND THOUSANDS

Spread fresh slices of both brown and white bread lightly with butter. Top with a generous amount of rainbow sprinkles (called hundreds and thousands in Australia), cut into dainty sizes. Do not try to spread after you have put on the sprinkles, or the colors will run. Chocolate sprinkles are also enjoyed, although the expression "hundreds and thousands" is a term most often associated with very special occasions like kids' birthday parties.

TOMATO SANDWICHES†

Slice bread (the freshest possible—there's nothing worse than tomato sandwiches on one day old bread) as thinly as possible. Spread each slice with butter or margarine. Select a firm ripe tomato and slice very thinly. Place one layer of tomato on bread, sprinkle with salt and pepper to taste, close sandwich, cut into triangles.

†No, nothing has been left out. On occasion I ask for a grilled tomato sandwich at our university cafeteria, and always get the response, "You mean cheese and tomato?" Sometimes I ask for a BLT without lettuce, bacon, or mayo but with a little butter! It's an expensive way to buy it, but sometimes it's the only way I can convince the waitress (or she the chef) to get what I want! I am, though, mostly disappointed when the sandwich comes. The tomato is always cut too thick. To reproduce the Australian sandwich the tomato must be sliced very thin.

Tomato sandwiches are virtually the staple Australian food (excluding beer, that is). I wouldn't mind ten cents for each one I ate when I went to school.

OTHER SANDWICH FILLINGS

Try these fillings in your *small, thin* sandwiches. Remember to butter the bread.

diced asparagus
processed cheese and diced celery
tomato and cucumber
cucumber
sardines
vegemite and cheese
corned beef and pickles
apples and raisins
cheese and raisins
ham and mustard
diced boiled eggs and lettuce
german sausage and ketchup†
cold leftover spaghetti
cold baked beans
salmon
potted meat

†German sausage is the Australian equivalent to bologna sausage. The taste is a little more spiced, but the consistency of the sausage is very similar. Ketchup is called "tomato sauce" in Australia.

A few of these fillings may seem a little "yucky" to you, especially the cold spaghetti. Remember, these sandwiches have very little filling, less than $\frac{1}{4}$ an inch at the most. You'll be surprised how good it tastes.

Some of these sandwiches are not so good for school or work lunches. Cucumber and tomato tend to soak through the bread and turn it to slop. These have to be made and eaten quickly. (No problem there with my family!)

HAMBURGER WITH THE WORKS

Hamburgers are about as American as one can get, though the name obviously is not American. Now that a certain fast food chain has moved into Australia, the (almost) indigenous Australian hamburger is on the road to extinction, if this has not occurred already.

One of my American friends who went on a business trip to Sydney some years ago would no doubt applaud this Darwinian fate of the Aussieburger. This is because he thinks that they are the wrong color!

1	pound lean ground beef	1	onion finely chopped
1	small carrot grated	1	small can beets
1	egg		

lettuce, ketchup, tomato, fried eggs, hard rolls

Lightly sauté onion and carrot, allow to cool. In large bowl, thoroughly mix ground beef (called "mincemeat" in Australia), lightly beaten egg, onion and carrot. Press into patties and broil or fry according to taste. While this recipe is not especially different from any recipe one would find in an American cookbook, there is one ingredient that I sneaked into the burger that sets it apart, and ruins its color—beets. In Australia, beet root (as beets are called) rears its ugly, velvety-red head in many unexpected places. When my American friend ordered an Aussieburger, and replied that, yes, he would have it with the works, liberal amounts of beet root were inserted. Unlike other hamburger ingredients, such as lettuce or tomato, beet root won't keep to itself. It seeps everywhere, and colors most of the hamburger purple!

I'm with my American friend. I hate beet root in sandwiches for the very reason that it won't mind its own business. To be honest, I would not eat a beet root sandwich either, even though I know Australians who eat them regularly.

Next page please...

A final difference between Australian and American hamburgers is that traditional Aussieburgers always used hard rolls, or at least they did in the old days (when I used to buy them at the late night stands on Saturdays in downtown Melbourne). Now that the fast food chains have moved in, all this is changing, since the hamburgers at these places, as far as I can tell, are exactly the same as here. By the way, these are the only sandwiches that Australians *don't* put butter on. Cheese was also never used in hamburgers, although fried eggs have always been popular.

SALAD ROLLS

On the few occasions when I used to buy my lunch at school, I would look forward to a salad roll (*without* beet root, thank you!). These rolls are simple to make, and today, because they have nothing but vegetables in them might be rejected as the food of health food nuts. As simple as the ingredients seem, these rolls are delicious. Because of my prejudice against beet root, I have left it off the list. But there are a lot of Australians who just love these rolls with lavish amounts of this all-embracing vegetable.

fresh crisp lettuce
thinly sliced firm tomato
grated carrot
thinly sliced cucumber
well chopped onion
thin slice of orange

These ingredients should be placed in hard crisp rolls that have been lavishly spread with butter or margarine. I have had difficulty finding rolls that are similar to those we used to use in Australia. The closest I could find was at our local Italian bakery. Add salt and pepper to taste.

GRILLED CHEESE

A grilled cheese sandwich is not the same in Australia as it is in America. This is because the word "grill" has a slightly different meaning. In Australian cooking, to grill food is usually to broil it. A grilled cheese sandwich is mostly done open style, so that the cheese melts into the bread and browns as well.

thick slices of bread
slices of processed cheese
butter

Place slices of bread under broiler and toast one side only. Remove, spread lightly with butter, cover with one or two (no more!) slices of cheese. Return to broiler and toast until cheese melts or browns on top. Cut into squares, serve immediately. This dish does not keep well. Cook and eat quickly. Popular in Australia for a quick snack or lunch.

On the difference between grilled and toasted sandwiches. A grilled sandwich in America is cooked on the hot plate, when each side of the sandwich is lightly buttered, then the sandwich is browned on the hot surface. The number of sandwiches in America that are cooked in this way are fairly limited: mainly to variations of grilled cheese, and sometimes with corned beef or ham. Grilled sandwiches as they are known in America are uncommon in Australia.

Scones

Grilled Cheese

TOASTED SANDWICHES

Toasted sandwiches, sometimes called grilled sandwiches (because "grill" often means "broil"), are very popular, especially for tea, if it is the family custom, as it was in mine for many years, to have the main meal at midday and light meal in the evening.†

We should also distinguish the Australian toasted sandwich from the sandwich that one might order in America, by saying something like, "BLT on whole wheat toast, please." In America, they toast the bread separately, then make the sandwich. In Australia, we make the sandwich, then toast the whole darn thing. All sandwiches may from time to time be treated in this way, but the out-and-out favorites are cheese, tomato and ham. I have even known some to eat toasted peanut butter sandwiches. Don't forget to butter the bread.

---

†If the terminology here is confusing, I'm not surprised. I have never quite figured it all out. We still call our kids in for "tea" which means to us, the evening meal. When we lived in Philadelphia, we once invited American friends to "tea." They arrived at the appointed hour (we had said 6.30 p.m.) having eaten a large dinner. They thought we had invited them for a cup of tea! I didn't find out till much later why they had pained looks on their faces when we served up a large three course dinner.

As far as I can tell, there is no set tradition in Australia as to which meal of the day is the main meal. There is certainly no European tradition of a big meal in the middle of the day. While motels for many years featured very large breakfasts (steak and eggs for example) this practice has largely died out. It is still likely that the main meal for most Australian families is in the early evening. This is mostly called "tea."

DAD'S SCONES†

Every kid who takes a home economics course in Australia is sure to have learned to make scones. For reasons I cannot understand, they are widely considered the most elementary of cooking skills. I have always found them very difficult to cook. There is a lot of folk lore about how to make scones turn out light and fluffy. I've tried them all, but mine more often turn out like—well—rocks. My father visited recently, and I made a point of getting him to give me a lesson. His scones always turn out great.

3	cups self rising flour	3	ounces margarine
1	teaspoon white vinegar	1	pint milk

Mix vinegar with milk to curdle. Sift flour, rub in margarine until mixture is like oatmeal. Add milk gradually and work with wooden spoon. Work dough until it becomes sloppy and sticks to the fingers. Sprinkle flour on board and knead dough until it is no longer sticky on outside. Pat out to about 1 inch thick, and cut with a glass dipped in flour. Preheat oven to 460⁰. Lightly grease cookie tray, and place in oven to warm a little. Place scones on tray, arranging so they almost touch. Paint tops with melted butter or milk. Place on top rung of oven, cook 8-10 minutes at 450⁰. My father says that the trick is to make sure your oven is very hot. Depending on your oven, you might even need to make it a little hotter than 450⁰. Do not allow to cool on tray. Immediately remove and place in, preferably, a wicker type basket, wrapped lightly in a thin cloth. Serve warm if possible.

---

†"Scone" rhymes with "gone" in Australian. I suppose it should be the same in American, although I have noticed that Americans usually say "scone" more like "cone." "Scone" also has other meanings in Australian. To do one's scone is to lose one's temper. One can also have a thick scone, which means to be thick in the head. As I have noted elsewhere (see *cookies*) a scone is almost the same as an American biscuit.

ELSIE'S SCONES

1	cup self rising flour	1	cup whole wheat flour
3-4	ounces butter	1	teaspoon sugar
	water		

Sift flour and sugar into basin and rub butter into mixture until it has consistency of oatmeal. Add water and mix until a soft dough is obtained. Tip out onto board and knead well. Roll out to about 1 inch thick, cut into circles. Place on greased cookie tray, bake 10 minutes in hot oven (400°). Wrap loosely in light cloth to cool. Serve warm if possible. Australians like them just with plain butter when served hot. If served cool, they are the number one item for an afternoon tea. In this case, serve in wicker basket and allow guests to open cloth to retrieve scone. Provide whipped cream and a range of jellies and preserves for toppings, if guests are seated at table. Otherwise break scones in half (don't slice—don't ask me why) and add toppings. Do not butter if you top with preserves and whipped cream.

VARIATIONS: Add 3 ounces of currants to the above mixture for delicious fruit scones. Alternatively, substitute for the sugar, 2-3 ounces of parmesan cheese for tangy cheese scones.

Elsie, my mother-in-law, played tennis at her church until she was in her seventies. Thousands of Australians play team sports over the weekend in various church and local groups. *Never* has it been known for any of these matches (games) to run without a break for afternoon tea. (Well, this is a bit of an exaggeration. They eat orange slices at three-quarter time in Aussie Rules football games, though I have it on good authority that some players do take a cup of tea at half time.) The scones in this recipe have fed hundreds of church-going tennis players.

CHEESE AND BACON SQUARES

1 cup grated cheese	$\frac{1}{2}$ pound lean bacon
1 egg	1 sliced sandwich loaf

Trim crusts from bread slices, spread lightly with butter and cut into squares. Mix cheese and egg well, then spoon on to bread. Preheat oven to 375°, place squares on cookie tray, and bake until golden brown. These are wonderful for breakfast ("brekkie" to Australians) and make impressive savories. Try freezing them and heat in a toaster oven for supper.†

---

†More confusion! I have never quite figured out how Americans refer to each of their daily meals. Is supper time the same as dinner time? And is it still dinner if you have it at midday? We always had Sunday dinner at home at midday. But we also had supper, as well as tea (that is, an evening meal). An Australian tradition when I was a kid was to have supper (more for grown-ups than kids because it was usually indulged in after the kids were in bed) late in the evening, not too long before turning in. The most common food taken at this time would be a round or two of toast, and of course a cup of tea, and for the more indulgent, a little soup. A touch of vegemite on the toast was also most welcome.

Australian sandwich   *American sandwich*

4

Steak, Chops and Snags

...grilled and pan fried meats

T he Australian Barbecue has become an institution. Most of the recipes in this chapter that call for grilling (broiling), could also be used for cooking on the barbecue (a "barbie" in Australian). It is by far the most popular way of cooking—especially entertaining—in Australia. The temperate climate makes it possible to spend a lot of time out of doors, which is where Australians like to be.

Get in lots of steak, lamb chops (the little ones with the curly tails that cost a fortune here, but are the cheapest in Australia), snags (sausages), a gas barbecue and plenty of beer, and you're set to entertain any number of easily satisfied guests.

Because meat has become expensive in recent years (not as dear as in America though), Aussies sometimes have a BYO (bring your own) barbecue. This means that you would bring your own meat, and the host would see that it was cooked right for you. You might bring your own beer as well. In fact, according to the rules of drinking etiquette, you *should* bring at least one bottle of beer without being asked, to show that you're not bludging (living off) others.

I once held an Aussie barbecue in, of all places, Rome, Italy. Each person was requested to bring their own meat. A Spanish friend showed up, very puzzled, with a dried pre-cooked packet of beef stew. Where on earth he managed to buy *that* in Rome, I don't know. I relate this story to show that, while we take the concept of a barbecue as self evident and very straightforward, to those from a different culture, they are very strange occasions indeed.

Roasts are also very common in Australia. However, I have included only one roast, that of roast lamb, because roasts are pretty much the same everywhere, and because I know that if I were to suggest to Americans that they roast their beef until it was very (and I mean very) well done, they would refuse to eat it. By and large, Australians tend to eat meat well done, at least old Australians do. There are, of course, many exceptions. My Australian friends will probably attack me for this unkind observation. (Unkind, because it appears the common view in civilized countries of the Northern Hemisphere that it is more cultured to eat meat rare. This view does not seem to take advantage of primitive man's discovery of fire.)

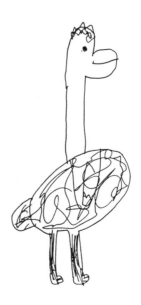

Emu

QUEENSLAND GRILL (BROIL)

4 slices choice steak†	2 small bananas
$\frac{1}{2}$ cup medium dry sherry	parsley butter
4 slices fresh pineapple	freshly ground pepper

Cut a pocket in each piece of steak and insert sliced banana. Pour a teaspoon of sherry in each, and close with a toothpick. Sprinkle with pepper and pour remaining sherry over top and allow to stand at least 4 hours. Place steak under broiler and cook to desired doneness. Just before serving place pineapple slices on top and heat briefly. Remove toothpicks and top with parsley butter.

PARSLEY BUTTER

Beat 2 ounces of butter, 1 tablespoon of chopped fresh parsley, pinch of salt and pepper into a smooth paste.

†Trying to match American steaks to Australian steaks is very difficult. Australian butchers cut their meat differently from American. I have found through trial and error that a large London Broil, as thick a piece of steak as possible, comes very close to the Australian steak in this and other recipes. I then cut the broil into slices of the thickness for the particular recipe.

About Queensland: This state was named by Queen Victoria in 1859, and is often called the "Sunshine State." Today it is a tourist resort and an attractive place for retirement. Bushmen of Outback Queensland had a different view:

Queensland, thou art a land of pests!
From flies and fleas one never rests,
Even now mosquitoes 'round me revel,
In fact they are the very devil.
But bid thee now a long farewell,
Thou scorching sunburnt land of Hell!

—*Bushman's Farewell to Queensland*, Anonymous, about 1870.

POCKET STEAK MELBOURNE

1 pound choice steak (2 pieces)	2 tablespoons onion, finely chopped
1 cup sliced mushrooms	2 ounces butter
salt and pepper	garlic butter

Trim any excess fat from steak, and cut a pocket in each piece. Melt butter and sauté onion and mushrooms until onion is transparent. Season with salt and pepper, then fill each pocket with mixture, sealing with toothpick. Brush steak with garlic butter, then salt and pepper, place steak under broiler. Quickly turn to other side and repeat procedure. Cook to desired doneness.

GARLIC BUTTER

Crush 1 clove of garlic†, add salt and cayenne pepper and beat into 2 ounces of butter until creamy.

†Among old Australians (in contrast to "new Australians" a term reserved for the thousands of immigrants who came to Australia after World War II under Australia's assisted immigration scheme) garlic is not a popular ingredient, because it is thought to upset the stomach, or embarrass the diner with an odor that lingers on one's breath. When we travelled on a crowded bus in the fifties, I remember my mother putting a handkerchief to her nose when we smelled this rich aroma. It seemed exotic and foreign to me then. Now I find it a necessary ingredient for many dishes.

One should not feel smug though. After all, my father loves to eat pigs' feet (called pigs' trotters in Australia) a dish that I have tried, but failed to eat. (The same goes for tripe.)

STEAK AND ONIONS

No country could lay claim to this dish as uniquely its own. Australia has its own version of this popular way to fix steak.

$1\frac{1}{2}$	pounds choice steak	$\frac{1}{3}$	cup plain flour
$1\frac{1}{2}$	cups breadcrumbs	2	eggs, beaten
3	ounces butter	3	onions, sliced
2	tablespoons milk		salt and pepper

Choose a thick London Broil for this dish, and cut it into thin slices. Dip each slice in flour, beaten eggs and milk, then breadcrumbs. Coat each side well. Melt butter and fry steak in pan. In separate pan, sauté onions until golden brown. Season with salt and pepper. Cook steak to desired doneness, then serve smothered with onions.

VARIATION: Cook your steak on a barbecue using a beer sauce.

BEER SAUCE

In a beer drinking country like Australia, what better sauce to baste your barbecue than one made of beer itself!

$1\frac{1}{2}$	cups tomato purée	1	can beer†
6	tablespoons Worcestershire sauce	$\frac{1}{4}$	cup cider vinegar
		1	teaspoon paprika
1	teaspoon salt	$\frac{1}{2}$	teaspoon pepper

Combine all ingredients and heat to a simmer. Brush over meat every 5 minutes until meat has cooked

---

†If you are cooking lighter meats such as pork chops or chicken, use an ale or light beer. If red meats are to be basted, use a dark beer, or to avoid sweetness, use imported Guinness Stout. To baste lamb, substitute rosemary for the paprika, and use a light beer. The size of the can is regular. If you simply asked for a can of beer in Australia, you would be given a large one which holds 26 ounces!

STEAK DIANNE

2	tablespoons Worcester-shire sauce	1	clove garlic (finely chopped)
	salt and pepper	2	ounces butter
$\frac{1}{4}$	cup chopped parsley		choice steak

Using meat mallet, pound steak until about $\frac{1}{4}$ inch thick. Rub in salt and pepper. Bring butter to a sizzle, toss in meat and cook in hot pan 1 minute or less on each side. Turn back to first side, sprinkle with half the garlic and parsley and cook for 1 minute or less, then do same on other side. Add Worcestershire sauce and cook 1 minute more. Lift steak onto serving dish, cover with sauce from pan. Australians like this dish served with a crisp salad (on the same plate! See: *Australian Salads*, page 70).

Steak Dianne is a universal favorite. One can hardly claim that it is an especially Australian dish. Yet, when one considers the early history of Australian foods—largely English in origin, which was to stick to plain and simple food, without any strong herbs or spices—Steak Dianne holds a special place. It was among the first of the more "spiced" or fancy dishes found acceptable by older Australians. These days, it is a popular item on many pub Counter Lunch menus.

FRUIT CHOPS MILDURA

6	pork loin chops	$\frac{1}{2}$	cup pineapple juice
$\frac{1}{2}$	cup honey	6	slices of orange
1	teaspoon mustard (optional)	$\frac{1}{4}$	cup brown sugar salt and pepper
6	maraschino cherries	4-6	whole cloves
6	slices of lemon		

Brown chops on both sides in buttered pan until almost cooked, add salt and pepper. Combine pineapple juice, honey, brown sugar, mustard and cloves. Place chops in large flat casserole, pour liquid over chops. Gently cook in oven preheated to 375⁰, for a further 10 minutes. Be careful not to over cook, or chops may become tough. Before serving, attach to each chop a slice of orange, lemon and top with cherry (use toothpick). Best served with boiled fluffy rice, and a dry white wine.

"Mildura," an Aboriginal word, means "red earth," which is certainly the color of the land surrounding this large town in the North West of the state of Victoria (the Southern tip of Australia). The area is renowned for its citrus orchards and vineyards. The use of fresh fruits, especially citrus and tropical fruits has become a distinctive part of Australia's cuisine.

To Australians, however, Mildura's main claim to fame is its *Workingman's Club* (built in 1938) which boasts the longest bar in the world. Pubs (hotels and bars) were prohibited in Mildura early this century, so private clubs were formed.

PRUNE STEAK

2	pounds choice steak		salt and pepper
1	ounce butter	$\frac{1}{2}$	pound prunes
2	tablespoons lemon rind	1	large onion, sliced
$\frac{1}{4}$	cup plum jam	1	teaspoon soy sauce
2	tablespoons vinegar	$1\frac{1}{4}$	cups water
3-4	peeled tomatoes		chives and parsley
$\frac{1}{4}$	cup flour		(chopped)

Slice steak into large squares, season with salt and pepper, pound with meat mallet. Sauté onion in large pan until soft; remove and keep warm. In same pan, brown meat quickly on both sides; remove and keep warm. Sprinkle flour into pan, brown, blend in water. Stir in soy sauce, vinegar and jam. Boil, stirring constantly, until mixture thickens. Return onions and meat to pan, add prunes and lemon rind. Cover and simmer gently for 30-40 minutes until steak is tender. Arrange tomato around in wedges and heat through. Sprinkle with parsley and chives when serving.

If you are still not convinced that steak has a very definite place in the Australian menu, an observation made by the childrens' story writer, Beatrix Potter will dispel any doubts:

> The shearers evidently work very hard...and they live very well—five meals a day, at three of which they have hot meat....they get...20 [shillings] a week, and rations—10 [pound] of meat, 10 [pound] of flour, 2 [pound] sugar and $\frac{1}{4}$ [pound] tea per man per week.

—Beatrix Potter in *The Webbs' Australian Diary*, October 9, 1898.

AUSTRALIAN MIXED GRILL

Because of the unavailability in this country of one of the ingredients of this dish (snags), we can only approximate the Australian version of a mixed grill. The required ingredients are:

choice steak (rump or porterhouse)
bacon
large (preferably wild) mushrooms
snags (sausages)
loin lamb chops
butter
tomatoes, halved

Whether grilled (broiled) or barbecued, this is a perennial favorite among Australians, a nation of meat eaters. Broil each item to the desired doneness. While meat is cooking, fry bacon to crisp, and sauté mushroom in butter. When meat is almost cooked, place tomato halves under broiler and broil till sizzling. Turn out on to plates prewarmed, placing bacon over lamb chop, and mushroom over steak. Australians like this dish with French fries (chips to Aussies).

Among certain hard working individuals who like a big brekkie, (breakfast) a mixed grill may find special attraction.

Unfortunately, we are unable to replicate this recipe because there is no equivalent in America to snags. The closest I have found are sausage links, but these are usually way too spicy, the wrong shape, and don't have enough bread in them. Australian sausages come in two sizes. Short and fat (usually pork sausages) and long and thin (slightly longer than a regular hot dog). They are always strung together, and the butcher has to cut them off the string. Because the sausage meat is mixed with bread to form the sausage, they simply do not exist in the United States. I think they would be illegal! But I dream about them at least once a week.

GRILLED RUMP STEAK

By "grilled" we mean "broiled." Cook your steak in your favorite way. I prefer mine done over a barbecue. The special part of this recipe is the sauce.

$1\frac{1}{2}$	pounds rump steak	2	tablespoons butter
6	shallots finely chopped	$\frac{1}{2}$	cup claret†
$\frac{3}{4}$	cup tomato puree	1	clove garlic
1	tablespoon chopped parsley		salt and pepper

Broil steak until done to your liking. Melt butter in pan and sauté shallots until tender. Add wine, puree, salt, pepper and garlic. Stir till boiling and simmer for 5 minutes. Serve over steak and sprinkle with parsley. Serve with *Joan's Pacific Salad*, page 77.)

---

†Any good dry red wine may be substituted, but for sentimental reasons, I'd be happier if you tried to obtain a bottle of Australian claret from your local liquor store.

Rump steak is the more common, budget steak in Australia, most often featured on "Counter Lunches" which are low priced meals that one can obtain in just about every pub. You won't get one in a pub with a sauce like this though. My Australian friends who visit us in America mostly admit that American steak is better than in Australia. I'm not sure what "better" means. Australian steak is cut from "range fed" beef, mainly. The difference in texture and taste is quite dramatic. American steak is more tender, and definitely sweeter.

JACKEROO CHOPS

2	pounds lamb chops	2	tablespoons plain flour
1	teaspoon sugar	6	tablespoons ketchup
4	tablespoons Worcester- shire sauce salt and pepper	2	tablespoons vinegar
		1	cup water

Remove fat from chops, roll in flour with sugar, salt and pepper. Mix all liquid ingredients together and pour over meat. Bake in a moderate oven (375°) about 1 hour.

A Jackeroo is a station hand, usually on a large station in the Outback. In folk poetry, he is often of "good breeding" and lives with the station hands in order to gain experience:

> When you get on to the station, of small things
>   you'll make a fuss,
> And in speaking of the station, mind, it's *we*, and
>   *ours*, and *us*.
> Boast of your grand connections and your rich re-
>   lations, too,
> And your own great expectations, Jimmy Sago,
>   Jackeroo.
>
> When the boss wants information, on the men y'll
>   do a sneak,
> And don a paper collar on your fifteen bob a week.†
> Then at the lamb-marking a boss they'll make of
>   you,
> Oh that's the way to get on, Jimmy Sago, Jackeroo!

—*Jimmy Sago, Jackeroo*, Anonymous.

†"bob" is slang for "shillings" used long before Australia changed to decimal currency. The amount here is worth about $1.50.

ROAST LEG OF LAMB

1 leg of lamb
potatoes peeled, cut in large chunks
whole onions peeled
carrots cut in large chunks
parsnips cut in large chunks
pumpkin cut in large chunks
mint sauce
fresh peas

Pre-heat oven to 350^0. Depending on the type of lamb, you may need to add oil. Australian lamb usually does not require it. Allow 25 minutes per pound of meat. Add potatoes, onions, carrots, parsnips, pumpkin about 1 hour before serving. Lightly boil peas. Remove roast from oven. Carve thin slices of lamb, place on preheated plates. Carefully arrange selection of roasted vegetables on each person's plate. Add spoonful of peas to each serving. Bring each plate to guests seated at dining table. Pass around rich brown gravy and mint sauce.

MINT SAUCE

2	tablespoons fresh mint	$\frac{1}{4}$	cup boiling water
$\frac{3}{4}$	cup vinegar	2	tablespoons sugar

Wash and dry the mint, finely chop. Pour over boiling water, add sugar and stir until dissolved. Add vinegar, stir. Serve in small jug with teaspoon.

Lamb is the "flagship" meat of Australia. It has been the tradition in many old Australian families to eat a roast dinner, usually roast lamb (but roast mutton or beef is also common) every Sunday, usually after coming home from church.

5

Casseroles and Curries

$\boxed{\text{C}}$ asseroles nestle very well into Australia's way of life because they allow for an informal eating style. By this I mean that they are most often cooked for occasions when there are large family get-togethers, or for social gatherings, where the casserole can be placed at center table, and dinner served in "smorgasboard" fashion. If presented in this way, they provide no difficulty for the American guest. But should they be served in a formal, sit down dinner style, then you may be in for a bit of a problem. In fact, any formal dinner makes for a problem for Americans eating in Australia.

The reason is that Americans don't hold their knife and fork properly. In an informal smorgasboard style, the American way of eating a casserole type of dish, using the fork in one's dominant hand, collecting the food onto the concave surface of the fork is quite O.K. But in a formal dinner, this is unacceptable because the knife must be held in the right hand (whether dominant or not) and the fork in the left. To make matters even more difficult, the fork must be held with the concave side *down* which means that there is a definite limit on how much food you can heap onto the fork.

Managing a plate full of casserole and vegetables requires a lot of practice. However, in some respects, casseroles are a good place to start, because usually there is enough food with some body or absorbent texture (potatoes are very useful). You can push food that might normally fall off your fork (peas, for example) first into the potato, then on to the fork.

Learning to use a knife and fork is easier with a casserole type food, because no cutting is required. Here is where Americans are often unfairly maligned. They have been observed holding the fork gripped in the palm of their hand, as though they were about to use it in an Agatha Christie murder scene! The fork must be held in the left hand, pointer finger running down on top of the fork handle, thumb to the side, other fingers curled around and under. The end of the fork pushes up against the palm of the hand. The concave side of the fork is *always* facing down. It takes a lot of practice to cut steak like this. I suggest you do it somewhere away from others, because I have seen a whole chop accidentally flipped across the whole width of a dining table when an unfortunate diner's pointer finger slipped off the handle!

The drawbacks to eating a casserole with a knife and fork are the juice and gravy. Fortunately, Australians don't mind if you use bread (spread with butter of course) to soak up the remaining gravy. You might even get away with mopping up the gravy with bread held in hand. The more acceptable way would be to place the entire slice of bread and butter on your dinner plate, then cut it up into small pieces with your knife and fork.

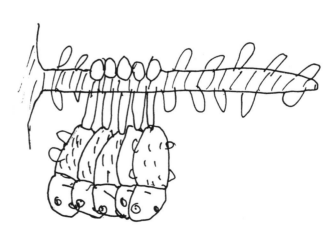

Aussie Possums

AUSSIE BEEF RAGOUT

$1\frac{1}{2}$	pounds cubed steak	$\frac{1}{2}$	cup beef bouillon
3-4	slices lean bacon	2	potatoes peeled and
2	onions peeled and		sliced
	sliced	2	carrots peeled and
1	cup peeled tomatoes		sliced
$\frac{1}{2}$	cup claret†	2	ounces butter
	salt and pepper	$\frac{1}{4}$	cup flour

Roll steak cubes in flour. Cut bacon into large pieces and lightly fry in butter. Remove the bacon then add meat and sauté until browned. Chop tomatoes into large pieces. Butter a casserole dish and place alternate layers of vegetables and meat. Combine claret and stock and pour over casserole. Bake covered for $2\frac{1}{2}$ hours in a moderate oven (350⁰). Boiled rice or lightly mashed potatoes are excellent companion dishes for this classic meal.

---

†Claret was probably the first of Australia's wines to receive truly popular Australian recognition (in contrast to international recognition, where Australia's wines of many types have done well in competition.) For many years, the Australian beer drinking tradition frowned upon the drinking of wine, a drink only imbibed by women and pansies. Australia's clarets are light and dry, excellent for drinking as well as for cooking! One can almost always find an Australian claret in a large liquor store. If you cannot, ask for a *dry* red wine.

HAMBURGER HOT POT

There are many Australian recipes that derive from the English "hot pot" recipes, of which there are many. Here is a variation that uses hamburger meat, and that seems to me very American.

4	potatoes, peeled and sliced	$\frac{1}{4}$	pound mozzarella cheese, sliced
2	ounces butter	1	pound ground beef
1	chopped onion	2	cups canned tomatoes

Melt butter and cook ground beef quickly over a hot burner. Add tomatoes, onion, salt and pepper to taste. Grease a casserole with margarine and empty $\frac{1}{3}$ of the hamburger mixture into casserole, then cover with half the sliced potato. Place another layer of meat mixture and cover with mozzarella cheese slices. Bake in pre-heated oven (350⁰) for 1 hour.

Echidna

BETSY'S PORCUPINES

$1\frac{1}{2}$	pounds ground beef	1	egg
1	small chopped onion	$\frac{1}{2}$	cup uncooked rice

Thoroughly mix meat, onion and egg. Make into small balls and roll in rice. Place in casserole and cook in a sauce of $\frac{1}{2}$ cup water and 1 can tomato soup.

VEAL AND PINEAPPLE CASSEROLE

$1\frac{1}{2}$	pounds lean veal	1	can pineapple pieces
2	onions, sliced		(reserve liquid)
4	ounces bacon (optional)	$\frac{1}{2}$	cup †tomato juice
$\frac{1}{2}$	cup beef bouillon	1	tablespoon parsley
	salt and pepper		(chopped)
$\frac{1}{4}$	teaspoon dried basil	$\frac{1}{4}$	cup flour

Be sure to obtain the leanest veal you can. If bacon is used, make sure it also is as lean as possible. Mix basil with flour. Cut veal into about 1 inch pieces and roll in flour and basil. Place half in bottom of well greased casserole and cover with half the bacon, parsley, onion and pineapple pieces. Add salt and pepper to taste. Repeat layers until no more ingredients are left. Combine $\frac{1}{4}$ cup pineapple juice, bouillon and tomato juice and pour over casserole. Bake covered for about 2 hours at 350⁰. This dish goes best with boiled rice.

---

†Pronounced *two-mah-toe* by Australians. I've never understood the inconsistencies of English pronunciation. If we say *two-mah-toe*, why don't we say *poo-tah-toe*? Instead, we say *pot-ate-oe*, just like Americans. My bet is that a long time ago, Ben Franklin saw how silly these inconsistencies were, and changed them!

SWEET AND SOUR LAMB

1	can pineapple pieces	2	ounces butter
1	large onion	$1\frac{1}{2}$	pounds cubed lamb†
1	cup diced celery	2	tablespoons corn flour
1	medium green pepper seeded and diced	2	tablespoons soy sauce
		2	tablespoons vinegar
1	teaspoon salt	$\frac{1}{4}$	teaspoon pepper

Drain pineapple pieces, make the syrup up to 1 cup of liquid with water and set aside. Sauté drained pineapple, onion, celery and pepper in half the butter until lightly browned. Remove from pan and set aside. Add remaining butter and cubed lamb to pan and cook until meat is brown on all sides.

Blend together corn flour, soy sauce, vinegar, salt and pepper and stir in reserved liquid. Add to meat and cook, stirring until mixture boils and thickens. Cover and simmer for about 50 minutes, or until meat is tender. Add pineapple and remaining ingredients and cook another 15 minutes. Serve over freshly boiled rice.

†*About Australian Lamb:* Lamb is probably the most widely preferred meat in Australia. To the visitor, Australian lamb has a strong, "gamey" aroma when cooking. After one has been in Australia some time, the nostrils adapt to this aroma, and one barely notices it at the many barbecues one attends. All countries have their own special and distinctive aromas. Australia's is of sizzling lamb chops and beer yeast.

Our local supermarket once or twice a year receives a shipment of New Zealand lamb, which is very similar to Australian lamb (not as good though!). If you plan to roast the lamb, you will not need to spice it with garlic and other herbs, because it already has a strong flavor.

SYDNEY BEEF SLICE

4	tablespoons tomato puree	$\frac{1}{4}$	cup evaporated milk
$\frac{3}{4}$	cup rolled oats	1	egg
1	teaspoon dry mustard	1	onion finely chopped
1	pound ground beef	$\frac{1}{2}$-1	cup grated cheese

1 4-serve packet instant potatoes

Mix in bowl puree, evaporated milk, oats, salt, pepper, egg,
mustard and onion. Using large fork and/or wooden spoon,
thoroughly blend in the ground beef. Grease an 11 by 7 inch
pan and spread mixture in base. Bake in pre-heated oven at
375^0 for 30 minutes. Make up mashed potatoes according to
packet directions and add half the grated cheese. Spoon over
meat, then sprinkle rest of cheese on top. Bake another 20
minutes. Serve with a brown gravy and traditional vegetables
that kids hate, such as broccoli or brussels sprouts. Kids love
this with ketchup. Men eat it with a bottle of beer.†

Ground beef in its infinite cooked forms is the food of people too busy to cook elaborate meals, or those with simple
and cheap tastes. Sydney is Australia's busiest bustling city,
epitomizing the contradictions of Australian culture. The fu-
turistic opera house sparkles, poised over Sydney Harbor; the
uncouth yahoos, larrikins and drongoes swill beer on the Hill
at Sydney's Cricket Ground.

†I say bottle of beer, because small cans of beer are uncommon in Australia. Beer is purchased by most Australians by
the large bottle or large can (26 ounces, usually in cases of a
dozen at a time). I have seen the large cans in many beverage
stores in the United States.

SPAGHETTI CASSEROLE

2 ounces butter	1 clove garlic
$\frac{1}{2}$ cup chopped onion	$1\frac{1}{2}$ ground beef
1 pound ripe tomatoes	1 teaspoon Worcester-
$\frac{1}{2}$ cup water	shire sauce
1 pound spaghetti	1 cup grated sharp cheese
salt and pepper	1 pinch oregano
butter	

Sauté crushed garlic and onion in butter until transparent. Add ground beef and brown well. Skin tomatoes (or substitute can of whole tomatoes), add to meat mixture with water (bouillon if preferred), sauce, salt, pepper and oregano. Cover and simmer about 15 minutes.

Cook spaghetti in boiling water for 8 minutes, or until tender but firm. Drain and turn into greased casserole dish. Top with meat mixture, dot with butter and sprinkle with grated cheese. Bake in oven at 350⁰ until cheese is melted and brown. Garnish with parsley when serving.

My Italian friends would shudder at the thought of this dish. But we ate many like it when we were kids. There are many kinds of baked spaghetti dishes in Australia, and we even eat it cold in sandwiches (see *sandwiches*, page 19).

BEEF STEW BALLARAT†

¼	cup flour	½	cup stock
1	large carrot, sliced	1	medium onion, sliced
½	teaspoon salt	¼	teaspoon pepper
3	slices bacon	2	pounds beef cubes
1	cup claret	2	tablespoons tomato paste
1	clove garlic, crushed	½	teaspoon thyme
½	cup mushrooms	1	bay leaf

Cut bacon into small squares and cook until crisp. Remove from pan and brown beef in bacon fat. Add sliced carrot, onion, salt and pepper, then flour, stirring to coat meat. Add bouillon, claret, tomato paste and herbs. Cover and simmer 2 hours. Cut mushrooms in quarters and sauté in butter. Add to stew. Serve stew with boiled whole potatoes topped with butter. Green peas are an excellent accompaniment. If you haven't finished all the claret while cooking, serve with the meal.

My mother and her generation never cooked dishes like this. In fact she never cooked with wine at all, as far as I can remember. Cooking with wine became popular with *my* generation, largely because Australian wines at last began to break through the beer barrier. Up until around 25 years ago, one would be thought to be a "sissy" or a "plonko" (skid row bum) if one bought wine in a pub. Beer was the drink, and a true Australian drank nothing else. Gradually, Australia's red wines gained a measure of acceptance, especially her clarets, and now wine is consumed in large quantities, red and white.

†Ballarat derives from the Aboriginal word 'balaarat' meaning resting place, bend in the river, is one of Australia's larger inland cities. It is chiefly known for its historical role in the gold rush years in the 1850s. The Ballarat gold fields yielded about $200 million, and one of the world's largest natural gold nuggets was found here—the *Welcome Nugget*.

IRISH STEW

1	pound chuck steak	$\frac{1}{2}$	pound onions
1	carrot	2	pounds potatoes
	salt and pepper		chopped parsley
$\frac{1}{2}$	pint water	1	parsnip

Trim fat from meat, cut into 1 inch squares. Place in pan with salt and pepper and cover with water. Peel carrots and onions and cut into slices, add to pan. Bring to boil and simmer for half an hour. Wash and peel potatoes, cut into large pieces and place on top of stew. Sprinkle with salt (if preferred) place lid on and simmer for 1 hour. Remove any excess fat and serve on plate with meat in center and potatoes all around. Sprinkle with chopped parsley when serving. This dish is excellent for cheap cuts of meat.

My mother may not have cooked stews with wine, but she did cook Irish Stew. It is well known that Australia was first settled by convicts. Many of these convicts were Irish (the Irish were convicted at a much higher rate than other social groups in England in the 18th century). Australians can therefore claim, with some degree of emotional commitment, Irish stew to be an important part of their heritage. Furthermore, it was an Irishman, Lalor, who led Australia's only violent revolt at the Eureka Stockade, near Ballarat in 1854. He was also assisted in this revolt by one American, James McGill. The gold miners demonstrated against excessive mining license fees, police brutality and many other matters that made life on the gold fields a severe hardship. About 1,000 miners barricaded themselves in the stockade on December 1, 1854. They were charged by 187 government troops (11 mounted on horseback). 30 miners and 5 soldiers were killed. The government changed its policies. Australians consider this to have been the nation's birth of democracy.

LAMB LEFTOVERS

1	green pepper	1	onion
1-2	cups prepared stuffing mix	1	egg
1	teaspoon Worcestershire sauce	6	slices lean bacon
1	pound minced cooked lamb		

Place green pepper in cold water and bring to boil. Let stand for 3 minutes, then core and chop finely. Combine minced lamb, chopped pepper, chopped onion and stuffing mix, then bind with egg and sauce. Form into round patty shapes about 1 inch thick. Wrap bacon around edges of patties, secure with tooth pick. Place on cookie tray. Heat in moderate oven 350⁰ until bacon is crisp and onion browned.

In America there are many recipes for left over chicken and turkey, because these are very popular everyday foods. In Australia, the everyday popular food is lamb, so what to do with lamb leftovers? Be careful not to over cook this dish, or the lamb will have that "cooked twice" taste.

Leftovers are the food that a *Sundowner* would be offered. A *Sundowner* was a vagabond in the late 19th century who constantly walked from one settlement to another, just arriving at a homestead at sundown—in time to eat, but not in time to do chores. There were also many sundowners during the 1930s during the Great Depression. More colorful were the *Swaggies* who "humped their bluey"—carried their belongings rolled up in a blanket, often with a billy (bush kettle, see page 147) hanging from the side—from homestead to homestead asking to work in exchange for a good meal. The sense of mateship and freedom these nomadic men had has been recorded in many bush ballads. The most famous of these is *Waltzing Matilda* in which a swagman commits suicide rather than lose his freedom:

And his ghost may be heard as you pass by that
    billabong
"You'll come a waltzing Matilda with me!"

—*Waltzing Matilda*, A. B.("Banjo") Paterson, about 1905.

SEA PIE

This special brown stew has a delicious upper crust topping with a scone-like consistency.

UPPER CRUST

1	cup plain flour	1	pinch salt
$\frac{1}{2}$	teaspoon baking powder	4	ounces shortening
	water		

Sift flour, salt and baking powder, rub shortening into flour until mixture looks like bread crumbs. Mix slowly with water to make a very stiff paste, then knead lightly.

STEW

1	pound beef cubes	3	onions
6	potatoes		pepper, salt

Sprinkle beef cubes with salt and pepper, place in pan with just enough boiling water to cover. Simmer for 30 minutes. Peel onions and potatoes and cut into small pieces. Add to meat. Roll upper crust dough (above) into a round a little less than the top of the pan. Lay it on the meat, replace pan lid, and cook for a further $1\frac{1}{2}$ hours. When cooked, cut the upper crust in four pieces and place on a warm plate. Arrange the stew on a hot platter and place the crust on top.

I have no idea why this tasty stew is called Sea Pie, especially as it has nothing to do with sea food. Perhaps the upper crust reminds one of the rolling sea?

WALNUT CURRY

2	teaspoons curry powder	$1\frac{1}{2}$	pounds beef cubes
$\frac{1}{2}$	cup chopped onion	2	ounces butter
1	medium tomato	1	banana, sliced
	(peeled and diced)	2	ounces chopped walnuts
$\frac{1}{2}$	pint bouillon	$\frac{1}{2}$	teaspoon salt

Brown meat in butter and remove from pan. Sauté onion and curry powder for 3 minutes; add banana, tomato, walnuts and beef. Cover with bouillon, add salt and simmer for $1-1\frac{1}{2}$ hours. When cooked, pour into large warmed tourine, decorate with walnut halves. Serve with fluffy boiled rice.

The Asian influence on Australian cooking dates well back to the beginning of the 20th century:

His cook was a Cantonese—Asian at least!
Who thought enough curry as good as a feast;
And his ex-soldier, from Antrim, named Barney,
Used to rowse the black stockmen in bad Hindustani.

—*Chillianwallah Station* by John Manifold, 1940s

CURRIED SPAGHETTI

4	ounces thin spaghetti	2	ounces butter
$\frac{1}{4}$	cup chopped onion	$1\frac{1}{2}$	teaspoons curry powder
1	pound ground beef	2	medium tomatoes,
2	tablespoons dried		peeled and diced
	mushrooms	1	cup tomato puree
$\frac{1}{2}$	cup beef bouillon		

Cook spaghetti in plenty of water for 8 minutes. Drain. Sauté onion and curry powder in butter until onion is transparent. Add meat and cook 5 minutes. Add tomatoes, dried mushrooms, tomato puree and bouillon. Grease casserole and preheat oven to 375^0. Place small amount of mixture in base of casserole, empty spaghetti on top, then cover with rest of mixture. Cover and bake 20 minutes.

Curried spaghetti! Boil it and then bake it! This is another dish that would shock my Italian friends. But Australians have strange spaghetti eating habits. They have eaten canned spaghetti for many years—even cold in sandwiches (see *sandwiches*, page 19). I honestly don't know any Australians who have eaten this dish (except myself). One thing is for sure: the recipe pre-dates the influx of Italian immigrants to Australia, and certainly owes nothing of its origin to India!

QUEENSLAND CURRY

2	ounces butter	2	onions, chopped
1	green apple, chopped	1	banana, sliced
2	tomatoes, skinned and chopped	1	tablespoon curry powder
$\frac{1}{4}$	cup flour	$1\frac{1}{2}$	pounds beef cubes
1	cup pineapple pieces		salt and pepper
4	tablespoons sultanas	$\frac{1}{2}$	cup coconut
		2	tablespoons lemon juice

$1\frac{1}{4}$ cups liquid from pineapple juice and water

Sauté in butter onions, banana, apple, tomatoes and curry powder. Add meat and brown. Add flour and cook 2 minutes, then add liquid, salt and pepper. Bring to boil and simmer $1\frac{1}{2}$ hours. Add pineapple pieces, coconut, sultanas and lemon juice. Simmer further 20-30 minutes. Check often for consistency, add liquid if necessary. Serve on bed of boiled rice. Make available an array of nuts (almonds and cashews), carrot sticks, coconut and celery sticks and apple slices to be eaten on the side.

This recipe is by far my favorite curry. Admittedly, one cannot argue that curries are Australian—naturally they are Indian. But my Indian friends tell me that curries with fruit such as this dish are rare in India, probably non-existent. There are also relatively few Indians in Australia, although there is a small old settlement in the North East of Australia. Australia is close to Asia and the Indian sub-continent and there are many Indian settlements throughout the pacific islands, with which Australia has traditionally had close contact.

YOGURT CURRY

1	ounce butter	2	onions, sliced
1	small clove garlic	$1\frac{1}{2}$	pounds beef cubes
$\frac{1}{2}$	teaspoon marsala	1	tablespoon curry powder
1	teaspoon tumeric	$1\frac{1}{4}$	cups beef bouillon
$1\frac{1}{4}$	cups plain yogurt		

Sauté garlic and onions in butter until transparent. Add steak and continue to cook until meat changes color. Now add curry powder, marsala and tumeric, and sauté 5 minutes. Add salt and bouillon, cover, and simmer about 2 hours or until meat is tender. Finally, add yogurt, stir well and simmer with lid off until most liquid has evaporated. Serve on bed of boiled long grain rice. Provide small dishes of chopped tomato, chopped onions, banana slices, coconut and pineapple pieces.

I was about 24 years old when I first tasted yogurt. Yogurt and other milk products (such as sour cream) were considered by the old Australians as somehow outside the realm of eating. My mother first tasted sour cream when she visited me in Pennsylvania. She complained that it was "off" (that is to say, sour), so we whipped up some fresh cream. It took me a long time to realize that cooking with yogurt was also O.K. I had been under the impression that yogurt was curdled stuff, and anything curdled had to taste bad. This dish is another one of my curried favorites.

6

Fish, Chook and Rabbit

A ustralia has an enormous coastline because it is both a continent and an island. One would expect a nation of fishermen and fish eaters. This is not the case. Instead, Australia has been, until very recently, a nation of sheep, cattle and wheat farmers. And the bulk of the population in the cities has eaten the foods they produced.

Today, it is the frontier land of the 80s, with new mining towns opening up in outback regions, and industrial suburbs cropping up everywhere. Fish consumption has not increased particularly, though that perennial favorite, fish and chips has steadfastly withstood the onslaught of American fast food chains. More chooks (chickens) are eaten, though, because mass farming and marketing of chickens has grown. Although there are many homes with chooks in their back yards, very few of these families would kill their own chooks for the table. It's easier to buy them, after all.

Rabbit is a fading food, I guess, though more prevalent than in America. Come to think of it, I don't think I've ever seen rabbit on the menu of any American restaurant, or in any food store. The reasons for the demise of rabbit as a common Australian food are many, some of which I'd rather not write about. The Australian government has sponsored many different attempts to reduce the rabbit population. Though still done, not so many people catch their own rabbits any more.

More importantly, rabbit has become less popular because chicken has become more widely available. I remember the few occasions we went to restaurants when I was a kid, and the grown-ups joking about whether a dish presented as chicken, really was chicken, and not rabbit in disguise. Rabbit was much cheaper and more widely available in the old days.

ABOUT AUSSIE CHIPS (FRENCH FRIES)

Fish and Chips are represented to Americans as an English invention, which I suppose they are. However, just as spaghetti has been re-invented by a number of cultures (China, Italy and America to name but a few), so have chips or French fries. The fact is that French fries taste different everywhere, except, that is, in fast food chain restaurants. There are important reasons for this, and important eating traditions that go along with these different types of French fries.

In Australia there are shops devoted entirely and only to selling fish and chips. While some might provide seating, it is generally expected that you will take your fish and chips out.

There are probably no fish and chip shops in Australia that are either owned or run by Pommies (i.e. English). They are invariably owned by "new Australians," — Australia's more recent immigrants, generally of Mediterranean origin.

A true Aussie chip is not crisp or thin, as in French fries sold in certain American fast food restaurants (now also in Australia). The potatoes in those French fries have been frozen, and for potatoes to be frozen they have to be a special kind of potato which is low in water content. Their taste is, if you'll forgive me, sterile—although the texture is acceptable.

Aussie chips are partially fried a day or two ahead of time. If you visit a fish and chip shop, you will see mounds of these partially cooked chips. This has the effect of changing the consistency of the potato to a much smoother, less powdery texture. It also conserves the potato flavor (along with the particular oil used for deep frying). When you ask for "A dollar's worth of chips," it is these that the cook will scoop up and deep fry in a matter of minutes. He will then (if it is a true, traditional fish and chip shop) wrap these chips, along with their fish, in thick paper. This has the effect of making sure that nothing inside could remain crisp. Instead, the chips become soft and soggy, but also remain very hot for a long time. Kids buy these, tear a whole in the top, and pull out one chip at a time. The chips are about three times fatter than French fries bought in America. Years ago, before nuisance health regulations, fish and chips were wrapped in one layer of white paper, then in newspaper.

In any season, there's nothing like a pack of hot fish and chips with plenty of salt, and a cold bottle of beer!

Koala and baby

FISH AND CHIPS

$\frac{1}{2}$ pound fish fillets† $\frac{1}{2}$ cup of flour
1 pinch salt 1 teaspoon cooking oil
2 eggs $1\frac{1}{4}$ cups warm water
potatoes peeled and diced for French fries (chips)
cooking oil for French fries (chips)
cooking oil for fish fry

Sift flour and salt together and make into a mound. Make a hole in center and pour oil in, then stir with a wooden spoon, adding water slowly. Mix until a smooth paste is obtained. Separate whites from eggs and beat to a stiff froth, fold lightly into flour mixture. Wipe fish fillets dry with paper towel, dip in flour, then into batter. Heat oil in pan, add fish and cook briskly until golden brown.

CHIPS (French fries): Dice potatoes into desired shapes. Wipe off excess moisture with paper towel, fry in hot oil. (See *Aussie Chips*, page 56.)

Serve fish and chips with slice of lemon, salt, and a crisp salad (on same plate) of lettuce and tomato. Vinegar is very popular for the fish. *Never*, repeat, *never* pour ketchup on your chips. This is an American influence strongly resisted by true-blue Aussies!

---

†Whiting is probably the best fish to use, although the frozen whiting I have found in my local supermarket does not have the rich taste of Australian whiting. If you buy fish and chips at an Australian Fish and Chip shop, and do not specify the fish, you will receive the cheapest fish which is called "flake." This is actually shark, and it's delicious, tender and flaky (hence its name). Whiting are the most popular fish served in pub counter lunches, although a fish called "flathead," bountiful in the bays and coastal inlets of Australia, is also popular.

GRILLED (BROILED) FLOUNDER

Select large, whole flounder. Fresh flounder can be told by eyes being prominent and bright, firm flesh and an agreeable smell. If in doubt, don't buy it. Do not use this recipe for flounder fillets.

Wash flounder well, remove head if desired. It is unnecessary to skin this fish. The flounder is a flat fish with both eyes on one side of its body. Turn over so that underside (usually white in color) faces up and paint liberally with parsley butter (page 30). Place under broiler and cook for 5 minutes or until browning occurs. Remove, turn over carefully so that cooked flesh does not break, and repeat process for top side (usually dark in color). Cook until brown. Serve on large oval plate with chips (French fries), garnished with crisp salad of lettuce and tomato, and slice of lemon.

Grilled whole flounder is a popular counter lunch item. Australians like them so that they cover almost an entire oval shaped plate. A simple trick will make your eating of the flounder more enjoyable. Begin by eating first one side, then turn the flounder completely over and eat the other side. Taking a little more care with the fin area, this method makes the flounder an easy fish to eat without too much worry about loose bones.

Whole flounder tastes completely different from the flounder fillets I have tasted in America. The meat is richer in flavor, and the texture is more flaky, less stringy. When I was very young, my father speared flounder in the shallow waters of Corio Bay (just near Melbourne). He would take a long pole on the end of which was attached a small light, and a spear about 5 feet long. The flounder are attracted to the light (the dark early morning hours were his favorite times to fish) and when they come up close can be speared.

CRAYFISH SALAD

large Crayfish (steamed)
Sydney Rock Oysters
cooked medium shrimp
deep fried Tasmanian scallops (cold)
fresh garden vegetables for salad

Break open the crayfish by slicing down the middle. Scoop out meat. On a very large salad plate, arrange crisp lettuce leaves and place morsels of crayfish in each leaf. Arrange legs and shell for decorative appearance, perhaps surround or fill with scallops, and or shrimp. Place Sydney rock oysters (raw and on the shell) with half slice of lemon around plate. Add firm slices of tomato, celery sticks, orange slices carrot sticks to plate. Provide a small jar of cocktail sauce and small jar of paste from head of the crayfish (called "mustard" because it looks like mustard). Serve with fresh fingers of white bread and butter. A delicious, dry Australian white wine would be most appropriate. And for a special treat, try the oysters with a small glass of very dry sherry.

Crayfish are the Australian equivalent (almost) to the lobster. In fact their tails are airlifted to some American restaurants and sold as lobster. The crayfish is found in most ocean waters of Australia, though those I am most familiar with are taken from the cooler ocean waters in the Southern tip of Australia, near Bass Straight (the strip of water that separates continental Australia from its 6th state, Tasmania). Crayfish do not have the huge pincers that Lobsters from North America have, their shells tend to be very rough and jagged, and the pincers are longer and narrower. To make up for this, the rest of the legs of the crayfish probably have a little more meat in them than the lobster. They are equally as expensive as their North American cousins.

OTHER BATTER-FRIED GOODIES

POTATO CAKES (1)

$\frac{1}{2}$ teaspoon salt
$\frac{1}{2}$ teaspoon pepper
1 ounce butter

$1\frac{1}{2}$ cups self rising flour
$\frac{1}{2}$ pound boiled potatoes
milk to moisten

Sift dry ingredients together and rub in butter. Mash potatoes well. Mix with flour and milk to make a stiff dough. Roll out and cut into rounds about $\frac{1}{2}$ inch thick. Fry in hot pan until brown on both sides.

POTATO CAKES (2)

$\frac{1}{2}$ pound potatoes, peeled
batter (*Fish and Chips*, page 58)
oil for frying

Parboil potatoes. Remove, drain and allow to cool sufficient to cut into slices about $\frac{1}{4}$ inch thick. Dip each slice in batter, then fry in hot pan until golden brown on each side.

RICE FRITTERS

2 eggs
2 teaspoons parsley, finely chopped

1 cup boiled rice
salt and pepper
batter (page 58)

Beat eggs well, add rice, parsley, pepper and salt, mix well then mold into patties. Dip in batter (see *Fish and Chips*) and fry in hot pan until golden brown. Serve with warm spaghetti sauce.

VARIATION: Substitute 1-2 tablespoons finely chopped pineapple for parsley.

SEAFOOD PIE

CRUST

1   cup crushed crackers $\frac{1}{4}$ cup water
3   ounces butter, melted

Combine all ingredients until stiff dough is formed, then press into a pie pan. Chill.

FILLING

2   tablespoons celery powder   1   onion
1   can cream of $\frac{1}{2}$ cup small shrimp
    oyster soup†   3   eggs
$\frac{1}{4}$ cup milk

Sauté onion in a little oil, stir in soup. Remove from heat. Beat eggs and meat, add to soup mixture. Stir in shrimp and celery powder, and spoon carefully into pie case. Bake in moderately slow oven (300⁰) for 40-50 minutes.

†Australian families have very busy schedules, just like American families. Over the past 15 years or so, the number of families with both husband and wife working has increased at about the same rapid rate as in the United States. Quick meals become the order of the day, and ready made soups (the most common brand is *Heinz*) make these and some other meals in this chapter possible.

Flounder

FISH CASSEROLE

1	pound cooked smoked cod	1	small sliced onion
2	ounces butter	2	hard boiled eggs
$\frac{1}{2}$	cup cooked peas	1	small can sweet corn

Bone and flake cod and remove skin. Sauté onion in butter and set aside. Fold in all other ingredients, then the cod. Spoon into casserole and sprinkle with breadcrumbs. Bake in moderate oven (350⁰) until hot and topping is crisp.

SAUCE

2	ounces butter		cayenne pepper
4	tablespoons plain flour	$1\frac{1}{4}$	cups milk

Melt butter, stir in flour and cayenne pepper, and cook for 1 minute. Gradually add milk, stirring until thick.

SWEET AND SOUR FISH

$1\frac{3}{4}$	ounces butter	$\frac{1}{4}$	cup flour
1	cup cooked peas	2	cups chopped celery
$1\frac{1}{4}$	cups milk	1	cup white vinegar
1	cup sugar	2	large cans tuna
1	cup (or less) cooked rice		

Melt butter in pan, add flour and mix to paste. On moderate heat, add milk slowly stirring until sauce thickens. Add vinegar and sugar, mix well. Fold in tuna, peas, celery and cooked rice, less rice if mixture is stiff. Place in greased casserole and heat in moderate oven (300⁰) until hot. Serve with fluffy boiled rice.

PERTH PIE

$\frac{1}{2}$	tablespoon mayonnaise	1	beaten egg
1	can salmon	$1\frac{1}{2}$	ounces butter
$\frac{1}{4}$	cup plain flour	$1\frac{1}{4}$	cups milk
$\frac{1}{4}$	lemon for juice		

Make a mornay sauce by combining butter, flour and milk to make a white sauce (see *sweet and sour fish*, page 63), then adding a small amount to the beaten egg, mayonnaise and lemon juice, stirring continually. Return this mixture to the rest of the sauce and heat well. Drain salmon and fold into mixture. Use juice from salmon instead of milk if stronger flavor is desired. Turn into a casserole.

CRUST

2	cups self rising flour	2 tablespoons butter
	milk	grated sharp cheese

Rub butter into flour until flour looks like oatmeal. Add milk and work until dough is soft. Roll out into oblong shape and sprinkle with grated cheese. Add cayenne pepper to taste. Cut into 1 inch pieces and place on top of casserole with cut side up. Bake in hot oven (400^0) until sour dough on top is golden brown.

Perth is the capital of Australia's largest state, Western Australia. It is named after the city of the same name in Scotland. What similarity the British saw between the two places puzzles me. They have nothing in common, but do have a big difference: the sun. We Australians tend to believe that, just as many Aussies have never seen snow, many British have never seen the sun! Perth is the sunniest city in Australia, with an incredible average daily sunshine of 7.8 hours.

CHICKEN CAIRNS SUPREME

2	pounds chicken pieces	2	ounces plain flour
2	ounces butter	2	slices bacon
1	large chopped onion	1	cup chopped celery
1	large can cream of chicken soup	4	tablespoons cream toasted almonds

Remove skin from chicken and dust with flour. Fry bacon and onion in butter until cooked but not brown. Arrange chicken pieces in casserole dish. Cover with bacon and onion and can of soup. Cover and bake 35 minutes. Mix through celery and cream, top with toasted almonds. Bake a further 10-15 minutes. Chicken or turkey leftovers may be used in this recipe. In this case, simply arrange leftovers in casserole, cover with soup, bacon and sautéed onion, and heat. Add celery and cream before serving.

Cairns is a large tourist city in the north of Queensland, gateway to the Great Barrier Reef, a coral reef of spectacular beauty, and thousands of miles long. The city was established in 1873 and named after the Governor of Queensland (1875-1877), Sir William Wellington Cairns. It is a city of particular interest to Older Australians and to Americans of similar vintage, for it was here that there was an important air base in World War II. Old Australians still remember the American presence in Australia and the pacific during World War II. The Coral Sea Battle was commemorated every year when I went to school in Australia. Many Australians felt then—I'm not sure whether this feeling continues today—that had it not been for the "Yanks" (a term of endearment as used by Aussies) Australia would have suffered badly in the Second World War. It was widely believed that the Americans saved Australia from a Japanese invasion.

Thank you America!

CHICKEN PIE

$2\frac{1}{2}$	pounds chicken	3	ounces butter
1	onion	$\frac{1}{3}$	cup plain flour
2	carrots	1	pound pastry
3	slices bacon	2	stems parsley
	bay leaves		whole black peppercorns

Pie crust: use pastry from *Mum's Pasties*, page 7. Place chicken in can with vegetables, bay leaves, parsley, peppercorns and about 2 inches of water. Bring to boil and simmer for about 1 hour. Strain off liquid and make up to $1\frac{1}{4}$ cups with water if necessary. Discard vegetables and herbs. Skin chicken and carve flesh into thick slices, removing all meat from bones. Melt butter and fry bacon, set aside. Add flour to butter and cook for 2 minutes. Add liquid, stirring constantly until it comes to boil, then cook for 2 minutes. Season with freshly ground black pepper, and salt to taste. Add carved chicken and bacon, cover and allow to cool.

Roll out pastry. Line large pie pan and pour chicken filling in pastry. Cover with pastry, and decorate with strips of pastry trimmed from edge, made into a lattice. Brush with beaten egg and cook in oven 375⁰ for 1 hour. Can be eaten hot or cold.

Chicken is not as widely eaten in Australia as in the United States, although it is becoming more and more popular. In my opinion, it's not as cheap as America either. When I was a kid, chicken was served as a real delicacy, usually on a special occasion. Turkey was unheard of. In fact I had never eaten turkey until I came to the United States. Chicken pies are not all that common. Certainly, they're no match for meat pies. One rarely sees chicken pies on sale in the store.

CHICKEN MARYLAND

chicken
bananas
potatoes
sweet corn
egg
seasoned flour
egg and breadcrumbs

Cut chicken into sections and par-boil. When cold, roll in seasoned flour, egg and breadcrumbs. Fry in pan until cooked and outside is crisp and golden. Cook potatoes and mash well. Bind sweet corn with egg and bread crumbs. Cut bananas into four and roll in egg and bread crumbs. Fry bananas and corn until golden brown.

SAUCE

4	tomatoes	$\frac{1}{2}$	onion
1	piece of bacon or bacon bone	1	teaspoon cooking oil
$1\frac{1}{2}$	teaspoons corn flour	$2\frac{1}{2}$	cups beef bouillon salt and pepper

Dice tomatoes, chop onion finely. Heat oil, and sauté onion until transparent, add tomatoes and cook 5 minutes. Add stock, bacon bone, salt and pepper, and simmer $\frac{1}{2}$ hour. Remove from heat and puree. Blend corn flour with a little water, then add to mixture. Stir well and cook another 2 minutes. Color and flavor with soy sauce if desired. Serve chicken pieces on large platter, with banana and corn arranged between pieces. Pipe mashed potato around edge of platter.

VARIATIONS: Substitute pineapple pieces or apple slices for the sweet corn. Instead of frying as above, dip chicken and accompaniments in batter and deep fry.

Next page please...

Chicken Maryland is no doubt an American dish, given its name. Yet this is one of the oldest chicken recipes one will find in Australia. It is also the most popular, and will be found on most menus of better pubs that offer a counter lunch a cut above the usual. The established popularity of this dish is all the more puzzling given that Australians, by comparison to Americans, do not eat a lot of chicken, and additionally rarely eat sweet corn. Come to think of it, apple or pineapple are more often than not substituted for corn. Only very recently have I seen fresh corn (called maize by Australians) at the green grocer (vegetable store).

Why chickens are called "chooks" in Australia, I have no idea. Keeping a few chooks in the back yard is a reasonably common practice. They don't cost too much to feed, they eat many of the nuisance pests (grubs) in the garden, their dung (in limited quantities) may be used for fertilizer, and they are a source of a few fresh eggs each day. Chooks also contribute to the rich sounds of Australian suburbia. Their constant clucking is a comforting sound, heard when one wanders through the fence-lined suburbs of city and small town alike. The day of sound is begun early with the cries of roosters from the back yards of hundreds of houses, and the warbling of magpies from the tops of lamp posts. In smaller towns, one is sure to hear kookaburras cackling in the evening.

APRICOT CHICKEN

	chicken pieces	apricot nectar (juice)
1	packet French onion soup	10 dried apricots

Place chicken into a shallow casserole. Sprinkle soup powder over, then pour on apricot juice. Cook in oven 320^0 for 1 hour. 10 minutes before serving, add chopped dried apricots.

CHINESE FOWL

6	small mushrooms	2	tablespoons Chinese gin
2	tablespoons soy sauce	$\frac{1}{2}$	teaspoon sugar
2	cups Chinese sausages (chopped)	2	Chinese pickled cucumbers (chopped)
$\frac{1}{4}$	teaspoon mixed spices	$\frac{1}{4}$	teaspoon ginger

Rub fowl over with soy sauce. Mix all ingredients and stuff chicken. Roast in oven 1-2 hours, depending on size of chicken. For an added treat, peel and slice potatoes as for French fries. Rub over with soy sauce, fry lightly, add to chicken half hour before serving.

Chinese Australian? You betcha! There is an old and well established Chinese community in Australia, most having come to Australia during the gold rush of 1851. (Others, though, were imported for cheap labor in Australia's sugar cane state, Queensland, also in the 19th century). Before the tremendous immigration of European and Mediterranean peoples after World War II who brought with them many wonderful cooking traditions, Chinese food was widely established. "Dim Sims" (dim sun in America) can be bought as take-out food almost everywhere.

> Celestial is the way he works
> The frying-pan and pot.
> A splendid feed can be produced
> While you'd be counting three,
> By the Mandarin from China
> That keeps company with me.

—*The Mandarin from China* by Alexander Forbes, 1869

DANDENONG RABBIT PIE

If you would like to eat rabbit but pretend that it's chicken, then this is the dish for you.

1	boiled rabbit	$1\frac{1}{2}$	cups chicken broth
3	tablespoons butter	5	tablespoons plain flour
$\frac{3}{4}$	cup evaporated milk	1	cup diced carrot
1	cup cooked peas		(cooked)
6	small white onions		bread crumbs
	grated cheese		salt and pepper

To prepare rabbit, see next page. Cut meat into small pieces. Make a white sauce using butter, flour, evaporated milk and broth. Fold in meat, carrot, peas and onions. Season. Fill oven proof dish. Cover with bread crumbs and cheese. Brown under broiler, then bake in hot oven (400°) for 20-25 minutes.

About rabbit: Rabbits are yet another gift from the English who settled our land. When I was a kid, rabbits almost ate Australia, there were so many of them. Many methods were used to reduce their population. One was to conduct a "rabbit drive." I remember one such drive, organized by a local church group, in which we began on a cockey's (farmer's) property, forming a long line of people, and made lots of noise. All the rabbits ran ahead of us, and were captured in a corner of the paddock surrounded by a rabbit proof fence. I can still see hundreds of pairs of rabbits hanging over the fence, and remember wondering who would eat them all. I'm still puzzled about that. I have not known many Australians who ate rabbit. In fact the only place that regularly served rabbit in my experience was the dorm I stayed in during College. I guess that figures.

About Dandenong, see page 90...

RAGOUT OF RABBIT

1	rabbit	1	onion
2	tablespoons flour	1	teaspoon salt
	pepper	2	cups water
	mixed herbs	1	slice bacon
2	tablespoons oil		

Wash rabbit in warm water and cut into sections. Roll in flour, pepper and salt. Peel and slice onion. Heat oil in pan, then fry rabbit on high heat, both sides. Set rabbit aside. Place onion in pan and fry with flour that remains. When brown, add water, bacon and herbs. Bring to boil, add rabbit then simmer for $1\frac{1}{2}$ hours.

To skin a rabbit: see page 145. In Australia it is possible to buy rabbits whole, or in pieces, deep frozen. Rabbit should be soaked in salt water before cooking, for about $1\frac{1}{2}$ hours to ensure that they are thoroughly clean. After soaking, wash with clean water, and cut off tail and a little of the backbone. Many rabbit dishes use bacon. This is not to mask the flavor (which is succulent, and similar to chicken, if well cooked), but to make up for the extreme leanness of rabbit flesh. It is a healthy meat, by all accounts.

RABBIT MUSHROOM CASSEROLE

1 rabbit	4 ounces bacon
2 ounces butter	$\frac{1}{2}$ cup mushrooms
1 tablespoon flour	2 tablespoons tomato
1 tablespoon parsley	paste
(chopped)	$\frac{1}{4}$ cup grated cheese
salt and pepper	1 cup chicken broth

To prepare rabbit: see page 71. Cut rabbit into serving portions. Melt butter in a pan. Roll rabbit pieces in salt, pepper and flour. Fry in butter until brown, both sides. Allow to cool, then wrap each piece in bacon, securing with a tooth pick.

Empty into casserole, add chicken broth, tomato paste and sliced mushrooms. Cook in moderate oven (350°) for 2 hours. If needed, thicken juice with a little corn flour and arrowroot. Serve topped with grated cheese and parsley.

As cute as rabbits are, they have been a serious pest just about everywhere in Australia. They have competed for the limited amount of grass with Australia's sheep (who have traditionally had first priority), not to mention Australia's indigenous grass eaters, the kangaroos. There are also hares in Australia, though not so many (see *jugged hare*, page 145). These tend to be much larger than the common gray rabbit, usually more tan in color.

We also went rabbiting with ferrets, ferocious little beasts. As kids, our job was to locate all the exits of the rabbit burrow. All but two would be blocked up. The ferret was put down one, and we waited at the other end for the rabbits to dash out, going at high speed. The challenge was not only to catch the rabbit in a net, but to catch the ferret, bent on destruction of its prey, and avoid getting bitten.

7

Salads

About Australian Salad

I t is not so much the conglomeration of different vegetables that makes the Australian salad so "typical" but rather the way the salad is served. This reflects a general difference in table manners between Australians and Americans. At our first Thanksgiving dinner many years ago, to which we were invited by some very kind Americans who saw that we were kind of lonely, we were fascinated to discover that all the wonderful food dishes were placed on the dining table, and passed around for each person to choose. The Australian tradition is quite different. All diners' plates are kept in the kitchen, where all food is served on the plates. These are then brought into the dining room and placed before the guests, just as in a restaurant.

The American practice of beginning meals with a salad is virtually unknown in Australia. The salad is usually eaten as a meal in itself, as described here, or kept to the side and eaten along with the main meal. My father, when he visits, is annoyed by this American practice. He keeps his small dish of salad, then empties it on to the main dish when it's served to him!

If you would prefer less formality (which is more Australian, actually) you might like to pack up your salad plates and head for the beach. In this case, choose your largest icebox (called a car fridge or "Esky" in Australia), carefully lay out the salad on separate disposable plates (strong ones so they won't absorb too much moisture and bend in two when you lift them out), cover with plastic wrap, and place in your icebox along with a plentiful supply of cold beer for the men (!) and soft drinks (soda) for the kids, and separately, a couple of thermos flasks of tea (for everyone). (Tea kept this way doesn't taste right unless prepared properly: see *cuppa tea*, page 132.) A few sandwiches and slices of plain bread and butter will also go down well. Then fill a container with a selection of cookies.

Now you're ready for a day on the beach. Load the boot of your car (trunk to Americans) with a cricket bat and ball, a large sun hat, and you're in for a relaxing sun-drenched day in the healthy salt air. I can feel the fine white and beige sand sifting through my toes...I see the gently swaying grass on the dunes...the sheer red cliffs facing the sea...

A day can pass by very easily swimming in the crystal water of Australia's surf beaches, playing cricket (see page 74) on the sand. These activities do wonders for the appetite—you need to have a big icebox. Australia is blessed with thousands of miles of sandy beaches, only a tiny portion of them "developed" in the sense that they are patrolled, have car parks and so on. Laws will not allow individuals to own or build up to the ocean shore line. Australians who travel abroad—whether to Europe or the United States—are aghast that one would either have to pay to get on to a beach, or that individuals could actually own land and houses right down to the water. The drive down Big Sur in California, while stunning in its own right, to an Australian seems defaced because of the houses (no matter how beautiful).

If you would like to serve your Australian salad in surroundings without sand but retaining the Aussie style, be sure to set your table with a "bread and butter plate" for each guest. Just about every Australian meal is served with bread and butter, Australian salads especially. The Australian bread and butter plate is about the size of a small plate that Americans would use for salad.

AUSTRALIAN SALAD

firm tomatoes thinly sliced
short celery sticks
grated carrot
thinly sliced cucumber
beet root
thinly sliced orange
thin slices of banana
one or two pieces of apple
fresh pineapple squares
fresh whole lettuce leaves
parsely
grated cheese
cold cooked peas
cold cooked string beans
small boiled baby potatoes (cold with butter)
sliced boiled egg
gherkins
pickled onions
canned salmon
raisins
potted meats

Use as wide a variety of fresh garden vegetables as you can find. The Australian salad is most often served with a few *thin* slices of cold cuts, such as roast beef, ham, German sausage or chicken, and a little potted meat (see *potted steak*, page 78). Naturally, these cold dishes are most popular in summer time, especially to clean up any left over turkey from Christmas dinner. The cold cuts are usually arranged flat on one side of the plate, nestling against various ingredients, with crisp lettuce on the outside of the plate. Thin slices of orange, split and twisted are common—intended to be eaten as well as for decoration.

VICTORIA SALAD

6 medium tomatoes
salt, pepper and sugar
$\frac{1}{3}$ cup grated cheese
1 tablespoon finely chopped pineapple and nuts
$\frac{1}{2}$ cup lettuce, finely chopped
1 teaspoon parsley, finely chopped
1 teaspoon chopped scallions

Cut off tops of tomatoes and scoop out centers, sprinkle with salt, pepper and sugar. Mash the tomato pulp well and mix in cheese, pineapple and nuts, parsley, scallions and lettuce. Fill cases with mixture, sprinkle top with cayenne pepper. Top with a small dob of thick mayonnaise. Set each tomato on a crisp lettuce leaf. Serve chilled. Don't forget the bread and butter.

GOLDEN SALAD

1 can pineapple rings
8 ounces cheddar cheese
4 medium tomatoes, firm
6 radishes
1 lettuce
French or Italian dressing

Cut the cheese into small cubes, the tomatoes into wedges, and radishes into roses. Tear lettuce into pieces and place in salad bowl. Arrange pineapple rings in circle, tomato wedges around edge. Place cheese cubes in center, radish rose in each pineapple ring. Garnish with a few mint leaves. Add dressing to taste.

JOAN'S PACIFIC SALAD

fluffy boiled rice
grated carrot
pineapple bits and some juice
currants
sultanas
chopped tops of scallions
cooked peas
chopped nuts (optional)
coconut (optional)

Mix all ingredients, varying amounts according to taste. Serve on large shallow dish, surrounded by orange and lemon slices. This salad is an especially good companion to sweet and sour dishes, casseroles with pineapple, and curries.

The influence of the pacific islands on Australian food has been gradual, but sure. The use of pineapple in many recipes is no doubt a product of Australia's proximity to the pacific islands and the fruit's abundance in the Northeast of Australia. I have eaten salads similar to this in Hawaii, although in the Pacific Islands the use of raisins and currants is less common.

POTTED STEAK

1	pound lean steak	4	tablespoons Worcestershire sauce
$\frac{1}{4}$	pound butter	$\frac{3}{4}$	teaspoon cayenne pepper
$\frac{1}{2}$	teaspoon mace	$\frac{1}{2}$	teaspoon ground nutmeg
	salt to taste		

Trim fat off meat, cut into small squares. Add all ingredients and steam in basin for 4 hours. Mince twice and mix into own gravy. Do not add water. Place in bowl, cover, and refrigerate. When set, may be used as cold meat sliced for salads. Or, may be used as a spread for sandwiches.

Australian menus do not often include paté, as known in French cuisine. However, the wide variety of potted meats available in Australia more than makes up for this gap. An exception is a product called *Peck's Paste*, a perennial favorite for a couple of generations. These pastes are sold in the supermarket, and there are many varieties, including fish paste, chicken, ham and other combinations. Their consistency and spiced flavor makes them not unlike their (distant) cousin, French paté. Needless to say, if used for sandwiches, the bread is always buttered, and only a thin spread of these pastes is applied.

8

Cookies and Slices

Cookies and tasty slices are made for all occasions in Australia, for entertaining, and to have around for the kids to stave off their constant hunger.

Australians have a casual lifestyle, and an enviable openness in their social life. A typical way to spend the weekend is to "drop in" on friends and relatives. This means what it says. One may be visited by people without warning. Many Australian households keep a constant supply of cookies and slices that can be produced, along with a cup of tea, for unexpected guests. An easy solution to this pleasant, but demanding custom, would be to serve bought cookies. However, as the English say, this simply would not do. The cookies and slices are often the focus of conversation, and it may be at this time that new recipes are exchanged and discussed.

Cookies are most often served in the morning at "morning tea" (around 10.30 a.m.) at which time everything stops. Most places of work sound a whistle or bell (I have seen this in factories, schools, universities and government departments) when it is time to break for tea.

ANZAC BISCUITS (COOKIES)†

My mother used to make these chewey mouth-watering cookies every few weeks, not especially on ANZAC day‡. I still dream of their treacle flavor.

$\frac{3}{4}$	cup fine sugar	$\frac{3}{4}$	coconut
1	teaspoon treacle	1	cup flaked oatmeal
$\frac{1}{4}$	pound butter	$\frac{3}{4}$	cup plain flour
1	teaspoon baking soda	2	tablespoons boiling water

In saucepan place butter, treacle, soda, sugar and mix with boiling water. Bring slowly to boil, remove and add dry ingredients, mixing well. Place large spoonfuls of mixture about 3 inches apart on well greased cookie tray. Bake in slow oven (275°) for 25 minutes.

---

†Not many Australians use the word "cookie." All cookies are "biscuits" to Australians. And what Americans call "biscuits" Australians call "scones" (see *scones*, page 24). Generally speaking, Australian cookies are drier and less chewey than American cookies. These are an exception.

‡ANZAC day is celebrated in Australia on April 25. On this day in 1915, the ANZACs (Australian and New Zealand Army Corps) landed at Gallipoli, and suffered the worst defeat in Australian military history. The fallen soldiers of all wars are now commemorated on ANZAC Day.

"Slouch hat" worn by
the ANZAC troops

AFGHANS†

In the Australian holiday season, (Christmas through New Year) ‡mums everywhere make these chocolate cookies. In a time when the abundance of chocolate can cause chocolate cookie blues, Afghan biscuits provide a distinctive chocolate taste that simply does not exist anywhere else.

$\frac{3}{4}$	cup butter	$\frac{1}{3}$	cup fine sugar
2	tablespoons cocoa	2	ounces cornflakes
$\frac{3}{4}$	cup self rising flour	$\frac{1}{3}$	cup plain flour
3-6	drops vanilla	1	pinch salt

Cream butter and sugar, add salt and vanilla to taste. Sift dry ingredients then add to mixture, mixing well. Add cornflakes and mix thoroughly. Place on cold greased cookie tray, and bake 15 minutes at 370⁰. These cookies are great plain, but even better topped with just a dolop of chocolate frosting (see *icing*, page 125).

†This is a very old recipe. I have no idea how these cookies got their name. They are a dark brown, however, and it's possible that someone in the outback who came across an Afghan and his camel, thought the cookies were the color of the Afghan (or maybe his camel). Yes, there are camels in the Australian outback. They were introduced in 1840.

‡This is not a misprint. "Mom" is spelled "mum" in Australian, and it can have other meanings as well as one's mother. If you are asked to "keep mum" don't tell anyone—it means to keep a secret. The pronunciation of 'mum' and 'mummy' is also different from the 'mommy' or drawn out vowel in 'mammy.' Aussie kids say 'mummy' or 'mum' using the short sound of 'u' as in 'hug.'

CHRISTMAS COOKIES

At Christmas time, Aussies always do their "Christmas baking" and prepare a variety of tasty morsels that are even more succulent than the usual fare provided at afternoon teas. Here are a few of the best, starting with my favorite, mainly because of the rum.

RUM FUDGE BALLS

1	can condensed milk (12 oz.)	$\frac{1}{2}$	cup coconut
2	tablespoons cocoa	1	teaspoon vanilla
1	cup plain cookies (crushed)	2	tablespoons rum

Use the plainest cookies you can. If you can find cookies sometimes called "English tea" these will be fine. Mix all ingredients thoroughly together, roll into balls. Cover with coconut, chill in refrigerator. Beer drinkers have been known to sneak these while no one is looking.

VARIATION: Take slivers of dates and encase them in the above mixture. Roll in chocolate sprinkles, chill.

CHOC BALLS

1	large pkt. marshmallows	2	ounces butter
6	ounces condensed milk	$\frac{1}{4}$	cup coconut
3	tablespoons cocoa	1	pkt. plain cookies

Use the plainest cookies you can find. Melt butter and milk very slowly. Add cocoa and coconut. Leave to set 5 minutes while you crush the cookies. Add to mixture, mix thoroughly. Roll into small balls, chill.

More Christmas goodies on next page...

APRICOT COCONUT BALLS

2 cups dried apricots 1 can (12oz.) condensed milk
1 cup cornflakes   1 cup coconut

Finely crush the cornflakes. Mince apricots and mix all ingredients well. Roll into balls, cover with coconut, chill.

COCONUT RUFFS

1 can (12oz.) condensed milk $\frac{1}{2}$ pound coconut
1 teaspoon vanilla   2 tablespoons cocoa

Thoroughly mix together all ingredients. Place teaspoonfuls on cold cookie tray and bake in oven 370^0 for 10 minutes. Keep refrigerated.

TUTTY FRUITY

1 can (12oz.) evaporated milk 1 passion fruit
juice of $\frac{1}{2}$ lemon   1 banana
juice of 1 orange $\frac{3}{4}$ cup sugar

Combine all ingredients, beat thoroughly and pour into flat pan, chill. Cut into small squares for serving.

Must I continue to apologize for our English heritage in cooking traditions? I'm not sure at which point one can claim that an adopted tradition can be claimed as one's own. Sometimes these adoptions don't seem to make sense. For example, when I was a kid, just about all our Christmas cards showed scenes of snow covered villages, families sitting around cosy fires by their Christmas trees. Hardly any Australians have seen snow, and Christmas comes right at the beginning of summer.

MINCE TARTS

These and many other types of cookies and slices are very popular in Australia around Christmas time—not often served during the rest of the year. Here is one of those recipes which happens to be my father's favorite.

FRUIT MINCE

$\frac{3}{4}$	cup chopped raisins	3	ounces currants
3	ounces brown sugar	$\frac{1}{4}$	cup mixed peel
$\frac{1}{4}$	cup chopped glacé fruits	$\frac{1}{4}$	cup shortening
2	tablespoons of brandy	1	grated apple
$\frac{1}{2}$	teaspoon mixed spice	$\frac{1}{2}$	orange
$\frac{1}{2}$	lemon		

Mix all ingredients thoroughly.

TARTS

12	ounces pastry	egg yolk for glazing
	fruit mince	confectioners sugar

Use pastry from *Amy Johnston Cake*, page 98. Roll out the pastry to about $\frac{1}{4}$ inch thick. Cut into rounds so that those for the bottoms are slightly larger than those for the tops. Line muffin tins with pastry, spoon in fruit mince. Wet edges of pastry cases, place on tops, and pinch together with sides. Glaze with egg yolk. Bake in hot over (450⁰) for about 10 minutes. Cool on wire rack and dust with sugar.

It happens almost everywhere, and has happened since the celebration of Christmas: an unfortunate tradition of over-eating and drinking. What drowsiness is brought on by the Christmas day sun!

Next page please...

MARSHMALLOW SLICE

6	cups cornflakes	1	cup coconut
1	cup plain flour	$\frac{1}{4}$	pound butter
$\frac{3}{4}$	cup brown sugar	1	pinch salt

Mix dry ingredients, add melted butter, mix thoroughly. Press with fingers into flat pan. Bake in moderate oven 350⁰ for 15 minutes. Allow to cool.

1	cup sugar	$\frac{3}{4}$	cup water
1-4	drops vanilla	1	tablespoon gelatin
1	cup choc. bits (melted)		(dissolved in hot water)

Boil together sugar, water and vanilla. Add gelatin, mix thoroughly, allow to cool. Whip until mixture becomes fluffy. Spread on cookie mixture and top with melted chocolate.

Stuffed with pudding to his gizzard
Uncle James lets out a snore,
Auntie flo sprawls like a lizzard
On the back verandah floor.
In the scrub the cows are drowsing,
Dogs are dreaming in the shade.
Fat and white, the mare is browsing,
Cropping softly, blade by blade.
It is hot. Mosquitoes whirring
Uncle James rubs his knee:
'Flo,' he whispers,'are you stirring?
It's near time to get the tea.'

—*Bush Christmas*, by David Martin, 1940s.

VANILLA SLICES

Vanilla slices are a perennial favorite. The center is a type of thick vanilla custard. I have found slices something similar in American bakeries, but the cream filling is not the same consistency, and as usual, there's too much of it..

4	ounces flaky pastry	$\frac{3}{4}$	cup milk
1	tablespoon sugar	1	egg
1	tablespoon corn flour	1	teaspoon vanilla

Use pastry from *Amy Johnston Cake*, page 98. Roll out pastry into 2 thin strips of equal size. Prick all over with fork and bake until crisp and golden in hot oven (about 400⁰). Blend corn flour with milk and sugar, stir continuously over low heat until boiled and thick. Remove, stir in vanilla and beaten egg. Spread between the 2 strips of pastry (you should have about $\frac{1}{2}$ an inch of cream between the two layers of pastry) and frost top with vanilla icing (see *icing*, page 126). Cool in refrigerator, cut into $1\frac{1}{2}$ inch squares.

These slices are hard to eat with composure, especially in Australia where it's not all that common at afternoon tea to be supplied with a dessert fork or spoon with which to eat these pieces of succulence. (Of course, one would receive the proper culinary implements if vanilla slices were served as a dessert at dinner, but this would be unusual). The problem is that when you bite them, the delicious cream filling oozes out the sides, making it difficult to manage one's teacup, saucer and plate and catch the dripping cream at the same time. Kids have no problem: they lick around all four sides first and gradually nibble away at the edges.

YO YO BISCUITS (COOKIES)

An expatriot dreams at least once a week of these addictive little cookies. My relatives cook these all the time, about as much as American Moms cook chocolate chip cookies or brownies. These are the blue chip of cookies. Once you have tasted them, you won't rest until you have devoured them all.

$\frac{1}{4}$	cup custard powder†	6	ounces butter
$\frac{1}{2}$	cup fine sugar	$\frac{3}{4}$	cup plain flour

Cream butter and sugar. Sift flour and custard powder 3 times. Mix into butter and sugar and work until a stiff dough is obtained. Roll into small balls about the size of large marbles, or a little bigger. If in doubt, it's best to be on the small side, as these cookies will be joined together with frosting. Place each ball on a greased cookie sheet, pressing down on the top of each with the back of a fork. Bake at 350⁰ for 15 to 20 minutes. When cool, join together in pairs with vanilla frosting (see *icing*, page 126). They look like yo-yo's! And they taste like nothing you have ever tasted before.

---

†Custard powder is a mainstay of every Australian kitchen. Hopefully your gourmet food store will stock this very useful product, made in England as well as Australia. Custard is easily made from this powder. In this recipe custard powder gives the cookies their distinctive, smooth taste.

WALNUT DELIGHTS

1 cup self rising flour	1 egg yolk
1 pinch salt	5 ounces butter
1 tablespoon fine sugar	1 tablespoon water

Rub butter into flour, add sugar. Mix to stiff dough with egg yolk beaten with a little water. Roll out thin and line greased muffin pans.

FILLING

2 ounces butter	$\frac{1}{2}$ cup walnuts†
1 egg	$\frac{1}{3}$ cup fine sugar

Cream butter and sugar, then add eggs and walnuts (finely chopped). Bake in moderate oven (325^0) for 15 minutes.

---

†Yes, it's true. There are no walnuts indigenous to Australia. They were imported into Australia by our English ancestors along with rabbits and other vermin. Fortunately, walnuts were one of the good things they brought. You could substitute pecans for walnuts if you prefer, although the result will be a slightly less zesty taste. Pecans are not often used in Australian cooking. Don't know why, because they're delicious—my wife has done her best to introduce pecan pie to our Aussie relatives, who clamored for more.

ANNE'S CHERRY RIPE

Cherry Ripes are one of the commercial candy bars that my wife dreams about, and which are unavailable in the United States. Here is a home made version given to us by our cousin.

$\frac{1}{2}$	pound plain cookies	6	tablespoons shortening
1	tablespoon fine sugar	$\frac{3}{4}$	cup evaporated milk
$\frac{1}{2}$	teaspoon red food coloring	$\frac{1}{2}$	teaspoon almond essence
$\frac{1}{4}$	cup glazed cherries	1	cup coconut

Grease a 7 by 11 inch shallow cooking pan, and arrange a layer of cookies in base. Melt shortening and mix in remaining ingredients, blending thoroughly. Spread over cookies and allow to stand for about 1 hour. Place in freezer, remove when frozen and cover with thick layer of chocolate frosting (see *icing*, page 126). When thawed, cut into about $1\frac{1}{2}$ inch squares.

There are a number of candy bars that are dear to the heart of every Aussie. We have tried, at times to reproduce them here, but with poor results. The two we adore most are made by the Hoadley Company of Australia: *Violet Crumble* a bar of honeycomb coated with milk chocolate, and *Polly Waffle* a hollow bar of milk chocolate coated cereal (something like rice crispies) filled with a light, fluffy marshmallow. We had most fun with *Jaffas*—chocolate balls covered with orange candy. They make a loud noise when dropped on the wooden floors of movie theaters.

DOT BOWMANS

The legendary Dot Bowman of Dandenong produced this recipe for my mother-in-law when we asked for a specially good cookie recipe for a cookbook our local school was assembling.

$\frac{1}{4}$	pound butter	$\frac{1}{4}$	cup sugar
1	cup chopped dates	3	cups rice crispies
$\frac{1}{2}$-1	cup melted chocolate		

Place butter, sugar and dates in saucepan and stir over low heat until a thick paste. Put rice crispies in large basin, add date mixture and stir well. Spread in a shallow pan. Cover with melted chocolate. Cool in refrigerator and cut into about $1\frac{1}{2}$ inch squares.

Dandenong is my wife's home town. It's nothing like the name suggests (a sleepy dusty village in the red of the Australian outback). Not at all. It's a bustling city, part of the suburban sprawl of Melbourne (located on the Southeast tip of Australia). Australia folklore authority, Keith McKenry, reports that "Dandenong" is aboriginal for "no good damper" which must be what aborigines many years ago thought of the cooking in this area! (See *Outback Cooking*, page 139, to find out how to cook damper).

"Damper wrong! Damper wrong!"
The toothless blacks all cried,
Excepting those who'd swallowed some,
And they laid down and died.
For what they'd gone and done, you see,
Though flour had been meant,
They'd gone and pinched a hundredweight
Of best Portland cement
Now over the years that mournful cry
Of *Damper Wrong* has changed,
And this is how the district
Of Dandenong got its name.

—*How Dandenong Got Its Name*, Keith McKenry, 1970

FROSTED CHERRY ROUNDS

4	ounces butter	$\frac{1}{3}$	cup coconut
$\frac{3}{4}$	cup plain flour	4	ounces fine sugar
2	tablespoons rice flour	1	egg

2 tablespoons crystalized cherries

Separate egg yolk and white, sift four and rice flour; add half the sugar and rub in butter until mixture forms a stiff dough with egg yolk. Turn on to board and knead lightly. Roll out to $\frac{1}{4}$ inch thickness. Cut into rounds with fluted cutter and place on greased cookie sheet.

Whip egg white stiffly and add remaining sugar and the coconut. Pile this mixture on to cookies and top with cherry. Preheat oven to 350^0, place in oven, reset oven to 300^0 and bake for 20-25 minutes, or until coconut is brown.

JEAN'S GINGER SLICE

This is another prize recipe from Dandenong (pronounced Dan-dee-nong—see *Dot Bowmans*, page 90). These slices will keep well, stored in airtight container in refrigerator.

$1\frac{3}{4}$	cups plain flour	$\frac{1}{4}$	teaspoon salt
6	ounces butter	1	cup fine sugar
$\frac{1}{2}$	cup preserved ginger	1	egg

Melt butter in saucepan and allow to cool. Add remaining ingredients, mixing thoroughly. Spread in shallow pan and bake in moderate oven (350^0) for 25 minutes. Allow to cool in pan, cut into slices.

MAY'S FUDGE SHORTBREAD

4   ounces butter $\frac{1}{2}$ cup sugar
$1\frac{1}{2}$ cups plain flour

Beat together butter and sugar. Add flour until mixture is firm enough to roll and put in shallow pan.

4   ounces butter $\frac{1}{2}$ cup fine sugar
4   tablespoons golden syrup†   1   cup condensed milk

Place all ingredients in basin and beat until creamy. Cook in small saucepan over medium heat, until mixture bubbles. Let cool, spread over shortbread. Allow to cool, then add topping:

2 ounces dark chocolate   1 ounce butter

Melt chocolate, add butter and mix thoroughly. Pour over mixture, allow to cool, then cut into slices for serving.

---

†Golden syrup is a byproduct of molasses manufacture and is hard to find in America, though should be available at your gourmet food store. I have substituted 1 part light and 1 part dark corn syrup with some success, although this mixture tends not to have the strong sugary-sweetness of golden syrup.

ORANGE FINGERS

4	ounces butter	6	cups coconut
$\frac{1}{3}$	cup condensed milk	$\frac{1}{2}$	pound plain cookies
	rind of 1 orange		

Heat butter and condensed milk over slow heat. Add to dry ingredients. Mix well, press into shallow pan, then top with orange frosting (use *lemon icing*, page 126 substituting orange for lemon flavoring).

RASPBERRY SANDWICHES

$\frac{3}{4}$	cup sugar	$\frac{1}{4}$	pound butter
2	cups plain flour	1	teaspoon cream of tartar
$\frac{1}{2}$	teaspoon baking soda	1	egg

Cream butter and sugar, add egg and beat well. Sift together flour, cream of tartar and baking soda. Add to mixture and mix well. Roll out thin and bake in hot oven (400^0) for 5 to 10 minutes. While hot, cut in two halves and join together with jam.

BURNT BUTTER BISCUITS (COOKIES)

2	eggs	1	teaspoon vanilla
$\frac{1}{2}$	pound butter	1	cup sugar
$1\frac{1}{4}$	cups self rising flour	1	pinch salt
	almonds		

Brown the butter, being careful not to burn it. Allow it to cool then cream with sugar. Add eggs, then vanilla essence, sifted flour and salt. Place small teaspoonfulls on cookie tray, and place half an almond on top of each. Bake 10 minutes at 375^0.

NEENISH TARTS

4	ounces butter	1	teaspoon baking powder
$\frac{1}{2}$	cup sugar	1	pinch salt
1	egg	1	cup plain flour

Cream butter and sugar, add egg and beat well. Mix in sifted dry ingredients and knead well. Roll out then line greased muffin pans with mixture. Prick with fork and bake 10-15 minutes at 350^0. Now prepare filling:

4	ounces butter	$\frac{1}{2}$	cup fine sugar
$\frac{1}{2}$	cup condensed milk	2	tablespoons lemon juice

Soften butter, add sugar, condensed milk and lemon juice. Spoon into patty shells. When set, ice top half with white icing and half with chocolate icing (see *icing*, page 126).

LEMON SNAPS

1	cup sugar	1	egg
4	ounces butter	2	lemons for juice,
	flour to stiffen		rind of one

Mix all ingredients together thoroughly, adding flour to stiffen to desired consistency. Roll out thinly, place on cookie tray and bake in quick oven (400^0) about 7 minutes.

ROMA'S CHOCOLATE VELVET

$1\frac{1}{2}$ cups finely crushed chocolate cookies
$\frac{1}{3}$ cup melted butter

Mix together and press into 9 by 13 inch flat pan. Bake at 325^0 for 10 minutes. Cool.

1	8oz. packet cream cheese	$\frac{1}{2}$	cup sugar
1	teaspoon vanilla (or less)	2	eggs
1	6 oz. packet melted chocolate chips	1	cup whipped cream
		$\frac{3}{4}$	cup chopped walnuts

Combine softened cream cheese, $\frac{1}{4}$ cup sugar and vanilla, mixing well. Stir in beaten egg yolks and chocolate. Beat egg whites until stiff peaks form. Gradually beat in remaining $\frac{1}{4}$ cup of sugar. Fold in whipped cream and nuts; pour over cookie crumbs. Freeze. After frozen, remove and cut into 1 inch squares for serving.

There's always a question of whether certain recipes are authentically Australian or not, especially because just about everyone in Australia (except the Aborigines, and even they came from Asia some 40,000 years ago) came there from some place else. Frankly, this recipe looks very American to me—the cream cheese is a bit of a give-away. But it's one that I've had for a long time, given to me by my brother's mother-in-law. It's so delicious, I couldn't resist including it.

NUGGETS NARDOO

4	ounces butter	$\frac{3}{4}$	cup brown sugar
1	egg	1	cup crushed pineapple
1	cup rolled oats	$\frac{1}{2}$	cup nardoo paste†
$\frac{1}{2}$	cup plain flour	1	pinch salt
$\frac{1}{4}$	cup chopped walnuts	$\frac{1}{2}$	teaspoon salt

Cream butter and sugar until light and fluffy, add egg. Drain crushed pineapple well, add to mixture. Stir in remaining ingredients until well combined. You may substitute $\frac{1}{2}$ cup flour for the nardoo. Place teaspoonfuls of mixture on ungreased cookie tray. Bake at 375⁰ for about 15 to 20 minutes.

†Nardoo is a plant, native to Australia, found in the Outback. It bears edible seeds, from which the Aborigines used to make a paste or dough. I have never met an Australian who has eaten this food, which is surprising because it is supposed to be an intoxicant as well! Nardoo is mentioned in many Australian bush ballads, such as that below which refers to Americans with the fond term (to Australians) of Yankees (no insult intended to Southerners, but Australians see America as totally north relative to their own position on the globe).

> No Yankee hide e'er grew outside such beef as we
>   can freeze;
> No Yankee pastures make such steers as we send
>   o'er the seas—
> As we send o'er the seas, my boys, in shipments
>   every day,
> From the far Barcoo, where they eat nardoo, a
>   thousand miles away.

—*A Thousand Miles Away*, Anonymous

9

Cakes

C akes, as with cookies, are kept in constant supply in the Australian kitchen. The necessity to keep cakes and cookies in supply is what sets the Australian kitchen apart from the American. It is usually cluttered with all kinds of containers for storing cakes and cookies. There are different containers for different cakes. Those with pastry in them should not be in completely airtight containers. Light cakes, however, such as sponges need to be completely airtight or they will dry out.

Cakes are most often served for "afternoon tea" which may be had anywhere from 2.00 p.m. to 4.00 p.m. While some work places stop for afternoon tea, it is not a common practice. Afternoon tea is more likely to be served to guests who arrive in the afternoon during a weekend visit. Usually, these guests are invited or expected guests, and baking is done specially in preparation for them. My mother liked to cook a tea cake just as our guests arrived, so that it could be taken out of the oven and eaten straight away.

Afternoon tea is not to be confused with the Scottish practice of taking "High Tea" on Sundays. This is a combined afternoon tea and evening meal, at which are served savories, eggs, toast, along with a variety of cakes and jellies. To my knowledge, high tea is not served in Australia. However, to confuse matters, the word "tea time" is used by many Australians, (myself included) to refer to the evening meal. We still call our kids to the table with this expression. They don't seem to be confused by it.

AMY JOHNSTON CAKE

Pastry, cake and jam. Put these simple favorites together, top with vanilla or lemon frosting, and you have a delicious cake that will excite the taste buds even of sworn beer drinkers.†

	Pastry:		Cake:
$\frac{1}{2}$	cup self rising flour	1	cup self rising flour
2	ounces butter	1	cup of sugar
$\frac{1}{4}$	cup milk (approx.)	2	ounces butter
2	eggs	$\frac{1}{2}$	cup milk

1 jar raspberry jam or preserves

PASTRY

Rub butter into flour, adding enough milk to make a fairly stiff paste. Roll pastry, place in flat pan and spread with jam.

CAKE

Blend flour and sugar, rub in butter. Stir eggs lightly, add to mixture, blend while adding enough milk to make a smooth consistency, easy to stir, but not too thin. Pour over jam and bake 25 minutes at 350⁰. Top with vanilla or lemon frosting (called "icing" in Australia: see *icing*, page 126), when cold. Cut into about 1 inch slices and serve with English tea.‡

---

†A genuine Aussie beer drinker (an "Ocka") would never admit to eating cakes or cookies. A real Aussie beer drinker doesn't eat sweets. He drinks beer and eats meat pies (see *pie 'n sauce*, page 8).

‡Well... there are lots of Aussies who, in their small rebellious way, now drink coffee—and be damned to the English! I've tried Amy Johnston Cake with American coffee, and can tell you it's terrific. However, if you plan to prepare tea, Australians are very particular about how it's made (whereas the English are more concerned with how one holds the cup!). See: *cuppa tea*, page 132.

MAISIE'S CHOCOLATE PEPPERMINT CAKE

$\frac{1}{2}$	teaspoon vanilla	$\frac{1}{2}$	cup sugar
2	eggs	4	ounces butter
$\frac{2}{3}$	cup self rising flour	4	tablespoons cocoa

water to mix

Cream butter and sugar. Add well beaten eggs and vanilla. Fold in flour and cocoa, mixing to a thick creamy consistency by adding water. Place in 9 inch cake pan. Bake in moderate oven (350^0) for 30 minutes. When cool, slice and insert filling. Or, better yet (my mother did this) cook another one, and place on top of each other, with filling in center.

PEPPERMINT FILLING

1	ounce butter	$\frac{1}{4}$	cup fine sugar
1	tablespoon hot water	1	tablespoon milk
3-6	drops peppermint essence		green coloring

Cream butter and sugar, add hot water, mix again, then add milk and green essence. Mix until creamy and smooth. Now a final touch. Cover the entire cake with a thick chocolate frosting (see *chocolate icing*, page 126).

MARSHMALLOW CAKE

Having lived in the United States for some time, I can understand why one would immediately assume that any cake or cookie with marshmallow in it would be as American as apple pie! The difference with this recipe is that you get to make your own marshmallow.†

1	egg	4	ounces butter
1	cup self rising flour	$\frac{1}{2}$	cup sugar
	rind of 1 lemon		

Cream butter and sugar, add eggs and rind of lemon. Fold in flour. When thoroughly mixed, press into flat pan and bake at 350⁰ for 15 minutes or until golden brown. When cold, top with the following:

1	tablespoon gelatin	1	cup sugar
$\frac{3}{4}$	cup water		

Place all ingredients into saucepan, bring slowly to simmer. Allow to cool, place in refrigerator for half hour or until quite cold. Beat until thick and white, add lemon juice to taste. Spread over cake, top with coconut.

---

†Marshmallow enjoys a warm spot in every expatriot Australian's heart. Most Australians have never seen snow, but they do know that the light fluffy marshmallow in "snowballs" (a ball of marshmallow dipped in chocolate, sprinkled with coconut) is whiter than snow, and is one of the memorable Australian lollies.

The word "candy" is not commonly used in Australia. Every kid asks for "lollies." Strangely, this word is often used in another context; "to shoot the lolly" is to lose one's temper.

SPONGE CAKE

In my mother's time, an accomplished cook was judged by how well she could make a sponge cake. These cakes are possibly the most typical of old fashioned Australian cooking. The recipes look simple enough, but be warned, it is especially difficult to achieve the light and airy consistency that sets this cake apart from all other cakes†. Here is one of my mother's favorites.

2	teaspoons baking powder	$\frac{3}{4}$	cup sugar
6	tablespoons melted butter	3	eggs
4	tablespoons milk	1	cup plain flour

Place in basin flour and sugar, break in eggs, add melted butter and milk. Beat 3 minutes, then stir in baking powder. Pour into 8 inch cake pans and bake at 375⁰ for 15 to 20 minutes. Sponges are typically served with jam and whipped cream in the center, sometimes with frosting on the top. My mother would cover the cake with thick whipped cream and decorate with strawberries. By all means serve this with a nice cup of tea! (see *cuppa tea*, page 132).

There are many stories that purport to explain the failures of cooking sponge cake. I still believe that slamming a door loudly at precisely the wrong moment while the sponge is in the oven will cause it to collapse, or fail to rise. There's no greater embarrassment than to retrieve from the oven, a flat sponge! However, thanks to another Australian favorite, there's something wonderful you can do to camouflage a fallen sponge...you can turn it into *lamingtons*. Read on!

LAMINGTONS

Lamingtons are by far the most popular of any Australian cake. They are found at tea parties and social gatherings—especially those of church groups. (Don't ask me why, but lamingtons are that close to being sacred it doesn't matter). The wonderful thing about lamingtons is that, provided one has the sponge one can produce these classics with hardly any effort.†

    1   slab sponge cake   chocolate frosting (page 126)
                       dessicated coconut

Use sponge recipe from page 101, and pour into well greased flat pan, so that mixture is approximately $\frac{3}{4}$ inch deep. Bake as before. When cake has cooled cut into approximately 1 inch squares. Prepare lots of chocolate frosting (see *chocolate icing*, page 126). Dip each square in chocolate frosting, then sprinkle all over with coconut. You won't believe how this simple recipe will send your guests absolutely nuts! And your kids who insist that they don't like coconut, will suddenly discover that they love it!

    VARIATION: Instead of chocolate icing, roll squares in strawberry or raspberry jello, and sprinkle with coconut. These are a little more messy, and you should plan on their being eaten right away (which they will be, for sure).

---

    †I have searched many bake shops in the American North East for cake that is similar to sponges, but have had no success. In Australia one can buy a slab of "golden sponge" which saves having to make the cake. I have tried this recipe with slabs of "plain" cake, and angel food cake, with reasonable results. It's hard to beat the real thing, but even this solution produces terrific cakes. These cakes are named after Lord Lamington, governor of Queensland, 1895-1901.

TEA CAKE

This is a light plain cake, often served with a cup of tea (see *cuppa tea*) in the afternoon. I used to hang around the kitchen and try to convince my mother to let me have a slice as soon as the cake came out of the oven.

$1\frac{1}{2}$	cups self rising flour	$\frac{1}{2}$	cup sugar
2	tablespoons butter	1	egg
$\frac{1}{2}$	cup milk		

Cream butter and sugar. Add egg, then milk and flour. Pour into well greased 9 inch cake pan and bake 25 minutes in moderate oven (350°). While still hot, rub butter on top and sprinkle with cinnamon and sugar. If there is any left the next day, try slices spread with butter, accompanied by a cup of tea, of course.

There is, admittedly, a question as to just how Australian this particular cake is. Tea cake is popular in England, where, after all, the tradition of afternoon teas originated. We certainly have a lot to thank the Poms for! "Pommies" or "Poms" are what Australians call the English. The word "Limey," common in America, is rarely used. In an Australian pub the English are more likely to be referred to as "whinging (pronounced win-jing) bloody Poms" which means that they complain all the time.

ORANGE CAKE

Australia's temperate climate ensures that there is a plentiful supply of fruit, mostly year round. Oranges and lemons are among the favorites. Lemons turn up in slices and fillings. Oranges in cakes.

2	cups self rising flour		rind of 1 orange
2	eggs	$\frac{1}{4}$	pound butter
$\frac{1}{2}$	cup milk	$\frac{2}{3}$	cup sugar

Beat butter and sugar together, add eggs one at a time, then orange rind. Add in milk and flour and beat for one minute. Bake 400° for $\frac{3}{4}$ hour. Top with orange frosting (see *icing*, page 126).

LEMON SPONGE

4	eggs	1	cup sugar
$\frac{1}{2}$	cup self rising flour	1	lemon
	juice of half a lemon		

Grate rind of lemon, extract juice. Separate egg whites from yolks. Beat whites stiffly adding sugar gradually. Add egg yolks and beat until thick and creamy. Fold in flour, rind and juice. Grease cake pan and place wax paper in bottom. Pour mixture into pan and bake in moderate oven (370°) about 15 minutes.

FAIRY CAKES

Children the world over love miniatures of all kinds. American kids love cup cakes, standard fare at birthday parties. Not to be outdone, Australian kids have their equivalent, with a little more fanciful name, Fairy Cakes. When I was little, my mother made lots of these, though the practice then was to serve them plain, or perhaps cut open and filled with a little raspberry jam. These days, it's unusual to see them without frosting.

$\frac{1}{2}$	cup self rising flour	$\frac{1}{2}$	cup corn flour
2	eggs		vanilla essence
$\frac{1}{4}$	pound butter	$\frac{1}{2}$	cup sugar

Thoroughly mix all ingredients together. Spoon into small muffin pans or into paper patty pans. Bake in moderate oven (320^0).

VARIATION: To make *BUTTERFLY CAKES*, slice top off each cake and cut the slice in halves. Top cake with red jello and whipped cream. Insert the two halves of the slice into the topping to make the butterfly wings.

FUDGE CAKE

1	cup self rising flour	2	tablespoons cocoa
1	cup crushed cornflakes	$\frac{1}{2}$	cup sugar
1	cup coconut	2	tablespoons golden syrup
5	ounces butter		

Melt butter and golden syrup (page 92), add to dry ingredients. Press into flat pan and bake about 10 minutes at 375^0. Top with chocolate icing (see *icing*, page 126).

DATE AND APPLE TEACAKE

2	ounces butter	$\frac{1}{2}$	cup sugar
1	egg	1	cup bran buds
$\frac{3}{4}$	cup milk	$1\frac{1}{4}$	cups self rising flour
1	pinch salt	1	cup chopped dates
1	grated apple		

Cream butter and sugar, add egg and beat well. Stir in bran buds, milk, sifted flour and salt, mixing all together lightly. Spread half the mixture in a greased pan and cover with dates and apple. Spread the remaining cake mixture on top and bake for 30 minutes at 370°. Cover warm cake with lemon icing and sprinkle with chopped dates and nuts.

BANANA TEA CAKE

2	ounces butter	$\frac{1}{2}$	cup sugar
$1\frac{1}{2}$	cups self rising flour	1	egg
1	banana	$\frac{1}{2}$	cup of milk
$\frac{1}{2}$	teaspoon baking soda		

Cream butter and sugar, then add egg, milk and flour. Mash banana and mix into ingredients. Bake in moderately hot oven (380°) for 25 minutes.

WHITE CHRISTMAS CAKE

4	ounces glacé pineapple	4	ounces glacé cherries
2	ounces glacé figs	4	ounces preserved ginger
2	ounces glacé apricots	2	ounces mixed peel
$\frac{1}{2}$	cup walnuts	2	tablespoons marmalade
2	teaspoons grated lemon rind	1	teaspoon ground ginger
$\frac{1}{4}$	cup sweet sherry	8	ounces butter
1	teaspoon vanilla	2	tablespoons honey
1	cup fine sugar	4	eggs
$2\frac{1}{4}$	cups plain flour		

Halve cherries and chop remaining fruit and walnuts coarsely. Combine in basin with honey, marmalade, lemon rind, sherry, glycerin and vanilla. Cover and allow to stand overnight. Beat butter until soft, add sugar, beating until light and creamy. Add eggs one at a time making sure to beat well after each egg. Add to fruit mixture, mix well and stir in sifted dry ingredients. Line a deep cake pan with several thicknesses of wax paper then spread mixture evenly into pan. Bake in very slow oven 270-300° for $2\frac{1}{2}$ hours.

Are these cakes truly Australian? I have to admit, I don't know. Yes, the tradition of rich fruit cakes, puddings and tarts using dried and candied fruits comes from England (which my father has always referred to as "the old country.") After all, Australia was settled mainly by the English, though later than North America. Captain Cook set foot on Australia's shores in 1772, around the time of the American Revolution. Thanks to the rebellious Americans, England had to find somewhere else to send her convicts, and Australia was it: an unintended byproduct of the American Revolution!

Thank you again, America!

CANDIED FRUIT CAKE DELUXE

6	ounces seeded raisins	2	eggs
4	ounces golden raisins	$\frac{1}{2}$	cup brandy
1	teaspoon baking powder	8	ounces whole cherries
4	ounces chopped dates	$\frac{1}{2}$	cup sugar
1	cup plain flour	4	ounces glacé apricots
6	ounces stoned prunes	$1\frac{1}{4}$	pounds whole nuts
$\frac{1}{2}$	pound glacé pineapple (coarsely chopped)		(brazils and almonds)

Sift the flour and baking powder then sift on to the mixed fruit and toss lightly. Beat the eggs with brandy and sugar until frothy; add to fruit mixture. Mix in nuts until evenly distributed and coated. Grease and line a deep pan and fill. Press down firmly with wetted hands and decorate the top with cherries and nuts. Bake in slow oven (320^0) for $1\frac{1}{2}$ hours and cool in pan.

While fruit cake addicts prefer their cake "straight" others may like the cake topped with a rich glaze.

APRICOT GLAZE

4	tablespoons strained apricot jam	2	tablespoons sugar
		1	tablespoon water

Place sugar, water and jam in small pan. Bring slowly to the boil and stir until sugar dissolves. Simmer gently for 2 minutes, then, while cake is still hot, brush liberally with glaze. Leave in pan to cool.

10

Desserts

A|ustralia cannot boast as many authentically Australian desserts as it can cookies and cakes. Some of its puddings are of course English in origin. However, their popularity is so strong, and they have been adapted to Australian ingredients in many cases, that it is reasonable to think of them as Australian. This observation applies especially to steamed puddings.

Two desserts deserve special mention, however. These are Pavlova and Peach Melba. They are special because they do not appear to be as directly derivative of our English heritage, and because they are named after famous stage performers who toured Australia at the turn of the century. Pavlova was a famous Russian ballet dancer, and Dame Nellie Melba a famous Australian opera singer. I would like to know whether there is any historical significance to the naming of these desserts after such people. Perhaps it could begin a tradition. One thinks of other famous persons...how about ...Reagan Roll...Pears Monroe...Thatcher-in-the-Pie ...need I go on?

It is often bluntly, sometimes gruffly, stated that real Aussie men (that is, the ones that drink gallons of beer, curse at the footy umpire (referee) and eat pies 'n sauce) don't eat sweets (an Australian term for desserts). This is a blatant lie. I have seen many of them do so, though rarely, it is true, in a bar. They couldn't do that anyway, because no publican (i.e. hotel keeper) in his right mind would even suggest such a thing, though he might serve sweets in the "Ladies Lounge" (see *drinks and drinking*, page 129).

FRUIT JELLY ("JELLO")

Australian kids call *Jello* and its equivalents "jelly." There are many variations of this recipe, but one thing is certain: jelly is a perennial kids' favorite.

2	packets jello (different colors)	$1\frac{1}{2}$	cups milk
1	tablespoon gelatin	1	tablespoon sugar
3-6	drops vanilla (to taste)		diced fruit

Australia is blessed with a temperate climate, so fresh fruit is abundant. Try to use fresh fruit if you can, but canned fruit (except pineapple) will do (drain before use). Prepare one packet of jello, mixing in diced fruit. Allow to set. Make white jelly by heating milk, almost to boil, and adding gelatin, sugar and vanilla. Stir until all ingredients are dissolved. Spoon on to fruit jello. Allow to set. Mix second packet of jello, pour on top. Allow to set, cut in squares to serve.

FRUIT SALAD

This is Australia's most popular summer time dessert. The abundance of fresh fruits ensures that this dish will never fail, and it's so easy to prepare. The serious host would go to the green grocer (a disappearing breed who is not green but rather specializes in selling all kinds of vegetables and fruits) and hand pick all fruits. These might include (but are not limited to) grapes, peaches, pears, apples, oranges, strawberries and bananas. The bananas should be added last and soaked in lemon juice before to delay browning. Add sugar to taste, though if you have selected your fruits carefully, there should be just about enough natural sweetness. Fruit salad is most often served with icecream. I prefer vanilla icecream because it does not overpower the flavor of the fruit. My kids, though, would go for either chocolate or strawberry.

PAVLOVA

In any season of the year at any party this renowned Australian dessert will be served. A kind of giant meringue, each spoonful of Pavlova instantly dissolves in the mouth. The wonderful thing is that, because Pavlova can be prepared in many different ways, one can always be surprised at a new and delightful variation.

Pavlovas can be difficult to cook unless you know a couple of tricks. *Don't* have the oven too hot. 275⁰ is plenty. *Don't* over-beat the mixture, or the egg whites will toughen, and the Pavlova will shrink too much when cooking. Pavlovas do not keep well. Plan to cook on the day you will serve it.

The variations in Pavlovas are achieved mostly by different fillings. The preferred fillings are mounds of whipped cream mixed with fresh fruit in some of the following combinations:

> sliced banana and passion fruit
> fresh raspberries and pineapple
> fresh strawberries and pineapple
> fruit salad (page 110)

If you're that way inclined, the addition of cordials (called liqueurs in Australia), such as cointreau, orange curacao or even a little cognac to the appropriate fruits gives the old taste buds an extra kick.

The greatest joy (after eating it) is the sight of the magnificent Pavlova rising up from the table like a huge snowball. Bombe Alaska pales into insignificance beside it. Because it's so popular and there are some important variations in cooking method, I have included a few of the most interesting.

Next page please...

MUM'S PAVLOVA

3-4 egg whites   1 cup fine sugar
 1   teaspoon vanilla   1 pinch salt
 2   tablespoons corn flour $\frac{1}{2}$ teaspoon cream of tartar
 1   teaspoon vinegar

Beat egg whites until stiff, add sifted dry ingredients, then add vanilla and vinegar. Line a large greased cake pan with wax paper, spoon in mixture. Bake in slow oven (275^0) for $1\frac{1}{2}$ hours. Allow to cool, fill with preferred filling.

ROSEMARY'S PAVLOVA

This recipe allows you to choose how big you would like to make your Pavlova, using relative quantities.

$\frac{1}{3}$ cup sugar to each egg white
 1   teaspoon corn flour to each egg white
$\frac{1}{2}$ teaspoon vinegar to each egg white
     egg whites
     vanilla

Beat eggs till stiff, then add sugar gradually, beating all the time. Fold in corn flour and vinegar. On cookie tray, sprinkle equal parts corn flour and confectioners sugar. Make a 2-3 inch circular collar of aluminum foil and place on tray. Spoon in mixture. Place in moderate oven (320^0) for $\frac{1}{2}$ an hour, then reduce heat to 275^0 for next hour. Top with favorite filling.

PAVLOVA CAROLYN

4 egg whites	1½ cups fine sugar
1 teaspoon vanilla	1 teaspoon vinegar
1 level teaspoon corn flour	

Beat egg whites till thick. Add sugar gradually (1-2 table-spoons at a time). Sprinkle in corn flour and beat. Combine vanilla and vinegar and fold into mixture. Place on wet brown paper on a cookie tray. Bake on bottom rung of oven at 275⁰ for 1 ¼ hours. This time, why not try a lemon filling ? (See *fillings*, page 128).

COFFEE PAVLOVA

4 egg whites	1 pinch salt
1½ cups sugar	1 tablespoon corn flour
1 teaspoon instant coffee	1 teaspoon vinegar

Place egg whites and salt in clean warm dry bowl and beat until stiff. Gradually beat in half the sugar adding to the mixture a tablespoon at a time, and beating well after each addition. Beat until thick and glossy. Now fold in remaining sugar. Quickly add corn flour, coffee and vinegar. On an up-turned 9 inch cake pan, sprinkle equal parts corn flour and confectioners sugar. Tie a band of greased aluminum foil around pan, leaving 3 inches above. Spoon in mixture, bake at 300⁰ for 1¼ hours. When cold, fill with ½ pint whipped cream mixed with 1 tablespoon coffee powder, 1 tablespoon Tia Maria or rum (if you must!). Top with grated chocolate.

CHRISTMAS PUDDING

Though it might be hot on Christmas Day, and some Australians have been known to have Christmas Dinner on the beach, there are few who would allow Christmas to pass without hot Christmas pudding. All Christmas puddings are a variation of what the English call Plum Pudding, although there are no plums in the mixture.

Christmas Pudding is a special favorite of both old and young. The grown-ups look forward to Christmas Pudding because it is terrific with brandy sauce (see *sauces and fillings*, page 125).

The kids can hardly contain themselves, because Christmas Pudding is always served with small coins (silver coins only, which in Australia are 5, 10 and 20 cent pieces) hidden inside! Yes, it can be dangerous, and I have known kids to swallow the 5 cent pieces (the smallest coin) who have been rushed to the doctor. But nothing ever happens, not even a tummy ache, and everyone tends to forget about the medical side of it—though these events are remembered and talked about for many years. However, if you decide to do this, it's probably best to issue several warnings to the excited diners, adults as well as kids. Also, in the olden days when coins were pure silver, or close to it, the coins were cooked right in the pudding. This is no longer a good idea, because the alloys in the coins will leave a nasty taste. Boil the coins separately, then just before serving, order everyone out of the kitchen, and wedge the coins into the pudding. With a little care, one can hide the coins so they cannot be seen too easily—although the kids are pretty hard to fool.

LIL'S PLUM PUDDING

3	cups plain flour	1	cup sugar
$\frac{1}{2}$	pound raisin	$\frac{1}{2}$	pound currants
2	cups boiling water	$\frac{1}{2}$	pound golden raisins
$\frac{1}{4}$	pound butter	2	teaspoons baking soda
2	teaspoons allspice	$\frac{1}{2}$	teaspoon nutmeg
	mixed candied peel		brandy to taste
$\frac{1}{4}$	teaspoon ginger	$\frac{1}{4}$	teaspoon cloves
1	tablespoon cinnamon	3	dates

Mix flour, sugar, fruits peel and spices in a bowl. Put boiling water in a saucepan with butter. When boiling add baking soda 1 teaspoon at a time. (Watch carefully, as it may froth over.) Mix the wet with the dry and put into a greased and floured oven-proof bowl. Make a lid of two layers of waxed paper, fasten with string around basin rim. Place in a saucepan and boil 4 hours. Keep level of boiling water about $\frac{3}{4}$ the way up the pudding. When cool, keep in airtight container in refrigerator.

Plum puddings are best made well ahead of time. They actually improve with age (we have made extra quantities and eaten them the following Christmas!). To reheat, place in boiling water as before, simmer for $\frac{1}{2}$ hour.

Christmas pudding is usually served with a small sprig of holly inserted in the top of the pudding after it has been emptied out onto a decorative plate. Allow your eager guests to choose from brandy sauce, brandy cream (see *sauces and fillings*, page 125), whipped cream or vanilla icecream as toppings.

If you're lucky enough to have any left over, sneak down to the kitchen early in the morning on Boxing Day (the day after Christmas), and cut yourself a thin cold slice. Fry it in a little butter, or simply eat it cold with a warm cup of milk coffee. Makes the breakfast of the year!

RED CAPS

Steamed puddings are *very* English, of course. Not to be outdone, though, we Australians have managed to produce a variation on the theme. Red Caps are little steam puddings, cooked in small tea cups, so that each person receives their own individual serving.

2	tablespoons butter	$\frac{1}{2}$	cup sugar
$\frac{1}{2}$	cup self rising flour	4	tablespoons jam
2	eggs		

Beat butter and sugar to a cream and add well-beaten eggs and flour. Put jam in four large tea cups (well buttered), and half-fill cups with mixture. Place in saucepan in 2 inches of water and steam for $\frac{1}{2}$ hour. To serve, tip out on to each plate. Great with whipped cream or custard.

GOLDEN PUDDING

2	ounces butter	1	pinch salt
$\frac{1}{2}$	teaspoon baking soda	$\frac{3}{4}$	cup milk
1	cup self rising flour	4	tablespoons golden syrup†

Melt butter in pan and add syrup, milk, baking soda, salt and the sifted flour. Mix well together. Pour into greased pudding basin and cover with aluminum foil. Place in pan of water and boil for 2 hours.

†As I have noted elsewhere (pages 92, 105), golden syrup is a popular cooking ingredient in many Australian desserts. Substitutes are difficult. For this recipe, you could try using the same quantity of marmalade, since there are quite a few other golden pudding recipes that exclusively use it and not golden syrup. My guess is that marmalade is the authentic English version of this popular pudding, and golden syrup is the Australian adaptation.

PINEAPPLE PUDDING

SAUCE

1	can pineapple rings	$\frac{1}{4}$	cup brown sugar
$1\frac{1}{2}$	ounces butter		

Cream butter and sugar and spread the mixture on the inside of a large greased oven proof dish. Drain the pineapple rings and place on top of mixture, cutting rings in half if necessary.

BATTER

3	ounces butter	2	eggs	
$\frac{1}{2}$	cup self rising flour	1	pinch salt	
1	tablespoon warm water	$\frac{1}{2}$	teaspoon vanilla	
$\frac{1}{3}$	cup fine sugar			

Cream butter and sugar; add eggs beating well after each addition. Sift flour and salt together and add to mixture along with water and vanilla. Spread batter over top of pineapple. Bake in moderate oven (375⁰) 35 to 40 minutes. Turn pudding upside down on serving dish, so that pineapple sits on top of batter. This dish is delicious served warm with icecream. If there's any left over (not likely) you can use it the next day as a cake. It cuts nicely into slices. Try it with a nice cup of tea (see *cuppa tea*, page 132) especially if you drink tea without sugar.

Pineapple was not often found in Australian recipes prior to the 1960s, even though it has been widely cultivated in Queensland, Australia's tropical north eastern state for many decades. Today, pineapple more than any other fruit sets Australian dishes apart from her English cooking heritage. Pineapple is most typical in Australian meat dishes (see *casseroles*, page 39).

MUM'S PINEAPPLE DESSERT

1	can pineapple	1	packet raspberry jello
2	eggs	$1\frac{1}{3}$	pints milk
		a little sugar	

Drain juice from pineapple, cut small and place in glass dish. Make a custard from egg yolk, sugar and milk, pour over pineapple, place in refrigerator and allow to set. Make jello (see page 110) from pineapple juice and jello. When setting, beat egg whites stiffly and fold into jelly. Spread over custard and allow to set. Serve with whipped cream.

HOPE'S SWEET

1 can unsweetened condensed $\frac{1}{3}$ cup fine sugar
  milk (chilled)   2 teaspoons gelatin
        2 tablespoons coffee essence or...
        2 tablespoons coffee cordial or...
        pulp of 4 passion fruit

Pour unsweetened milk into bowl and beat. Add fine sugar. Dissolve gelatin in $\frac{1}{2}$ cup boiling water and add to mixture when cool. Add your choice of coffee or passion fruit. Place in refrigerator and chill. Serve with chocolate mint wafers.

See page 127 about passion fruit. Coffee essence is unknown in the United States, though it is common in England and Canada. I have seen it in our local gourmet food store. Coffee essence has a distinctive taste, not especially like coffee (as we know it today). It was a special treat for us, as kids, to be allowed to have a cup of coffee made of coffee essence (1 teaspoonful in hot milk) instead of the regulation cup of tea. Coffee essence was always sold mixed with chicory, which is what gave it such a different taste.

PEACH TRIFLE

1	can peaches	$1\frac{1}{4}$	cups custard
$\frac{1}{2}$	cup peach juice	$\frac{1}{2}$	teaspoon gelatin
1	egg white		sponge cake (page 101)
	lemon butter		

Drain peaches and save juice, spread pieces of sponge with lemon butter (see *fillings*, page 126). Place †sponge cake in dish then sliced peaches and cover with custard. Dissolve gelatin in heated peach juice and when nearly set beat into a stiffly beaten egg white. Spoon on top and decorate with peaches and nuts.

VARIATION: Soak pieces of sponge in sherry.

†Sponge cake is not absolutely necessary for this dish, or any other trifle for that matter. In American cookbooks, trifles are usually presented as the most typical of English desserts. Yet again, I must admit that this dish, while not uniquely Australian, is nevertheless part of the cooking and eating tradition of Australians! One of the reasons trifles are such popular desserts is that the Australian mums cook lots of cakes. There is often cake left over, or lost in a multitude of containers kept for storing the many kinds of biscuits and cakes that might be available at any one time in an Australian kitchen, especially at holiday time. Trifles are most often made with such leftovers. We have found that trifles are very popular with our American guests. They are easy to make, yet one rarely finds them in American restaurants.

PEACH MELBA

This popular Australian dessert is made up in individual glass dishes. For each serving you will need:

> 1 piece sponge cake (page 101)
> 1 half large peach (fresh or canned)
> peach syrup
> sweet sherry (sprinkling only!)
> whipped cream
> pureed strawberries and/or raspberries

Place the sponge in bottom of glass dish, top with half peach, cut side up. Sprinkle with peach syrup and sweet sherry. Pipe large mound of whipped cream into center of peach. Pour strawberries and raspberries over peach and sponge. If preferred, place scoop of vanilla icecream in center of peach before adding cream.

This dessert was named after the great opera singer, Dame Nellie Melba, or at least so the story goes. It is popular in many Australian restaurants, and appears constantly in many different variations. Dame Nellie Melba was a legend in her own time. Just the sound of her name—a contraction of Melbourne, her birth place—sent people into swoons of adoration. Dame Nellie rose to success at the Royal Covent Garden in London during its golden years, and dominated the international opera scene from the 1890s till well after World War I. In 1914, she played one performance at Covent Garden before no fewer than seven kings and queens. In San Francisco in 1898, her rendition of *The Star Spangled Banner* in the music lesson scene of *The Barber of Seville* to a despondent audience at the height of the Spanish American war, brought the house down. On her international tours, especially to Australia, she was mobbed by screaming crowds in much the same way that rock stars are mobbed today. She accepted this as her due, noting, "There are lots of duchesses, but only one Melba."

APPLE CAKE

4	ounces butter	$1\frac{1}{2}$	cups self rising flour
1	egg	2	teaspoons cocoa
1	cup sugar	$\frac{1}{2}$	cup plain flour
$\frac{1}{2}$	cup milk	2	teaspoons cinnamon
1	cup apple sauce	1	teaspoon baking soda, dissolved in water

Cream butter and sugar, add egg. Sift flour and spices and add gradually, mixing well, alternately with milk. Add apples to which the soda has already been added. Mix in well. Cook in moderate oven (350°) for 40 minutes. Top with chocolate icing (see *icing*, page 126). This is a deliciously moist spicy cake. Plan to eat it the day you cook it, though, as it is does not keep well.

The cynical reader may have been waiting to come across an Australian recipe for Apple Pie, since I have included many other recipes that seem to be just as common in England as in Australia. But I couldn't be that brazen, even though Australia boasts a state, Tasmania, popularly called the "Apple Isle." There are Australian recipes for Apple Pie, but they do not vary from the American.

DREAM CAKE

$\frac{1}{2}$	cup butter	$\frac{1}{2}$	cup fine sugar
2	eggs	$\frac{1}{4}$	cup golden syrup†
$\frac{1}{2}$	cup chopped nuts	1	orange
$\frac{1}{2}$	cup raisins	$\frac{1}{2}$	cup currants
$1\frac{1}{2}$	cups plain flour	$1\frac{1}{2}$	teaspoons baking powder

Sift flour and baking soda. Beat butter and a little flour together. Separate egg yolks from whites. Beat whites, gradually
adding golden syrup. Add yolks then flour and butter mixture.
Beat in baking powder along with remaining flour. Fold in currants, raisins and nuts. Pour into well greased cake pan, bake
at 350⁰ for about $1\frac{1}{2}$ hours.

---

†See *golden pudding*, page 116 for notes on substitutes for
golden syrup. $\frac{1}{2}$ pound of brown sugar could be substituted for
golden syrup in this recipe. It will taste quite nice, but without
the golden syrup you will never know what dream cake *really*
tastes like.

I do not dream about these cakes, but perhaps the cre-
ator of this recipe did. The topic gives me a chance to mention the *Dream Time* in Aboriginal folk lore. According to
Gulpilil, a well known Aboriginal actor, the Aborigines, though
separated geographically into hundreds of completely separate
tribes in ancient times, believe generally that they originated
about 40,000 years ago. At this time, all animals were giants
that behaved like humans. Many stories tell of their exploits
which often explain how rivers were formed, and mountains
were made. This period is known as the *Dream Time*. At a
point in time unkown, and for reasons unknown, the giants
became humans and the Dream Time ended.

APPLE PANCAKES

1-2	apples	$\frac{1}{2}$	cup plain flour
1	pinch salt	1	egg
$1\frac{1}{4}$	cups milk	1	lemon
1	ounce butter		

Sift flour and salt, break egg into the mound of flour. Using a wooden spoon, gradually stir flour into the egg until it will take no more. Add half the milk gradually, until all flour is absorbed. Beat well until bubbles form. (If batter is well beaten, the pancakes will be lighter.) Stir in the rest of the milk, and allow to stand for $\frac{1}{2}$ hour. Peel and grate apples, fold into mixture. So that your pancakes will be thin, make mixture a little thinner than would be usual for American Pancakes.

Place a small piece of butter in the pan, melt, then pour out and wipe out with paper towel. Place another piece of butter in pan, and heat till quite hot. Drop large spoonful of batter into pan and fry until golden brown; turn with wide knife or slice. When cooked on both sides, remove and place on piece of paper. Sprinkle with confectioners sugar. These pancakes should be thin and large in size, so that they can be rolled up, and served on a hot plate. Serve with additional sugar plus a slice of lemon. They are delicious with lemon juice and sugar. Whipped cream is a bit of all right too!

It's hard to imagine how Australia could have anything new to offer America, the land of pancakes. But I have never seen apple pancakes like these in any American restaurant. Apple fritters—slices of apple deep fried in batter— are common enough, but they are unequal to the delicacy of flavor and texture of these apple pancakes.

PIKELETS
(DROP SCONES)

These are a variation of pancakes, but are smaller, thicker and a little heavier than the usual pancake.

$\frac{1}{2}$	cup self rising flour	1	pinch salt
4	tablespoons fine sugar	1	egg
$\frac{1}{2}$-$\frac{3}{4}$	cup milk		

Sift flour and salt, add sugar. Drop unbeaten egg into middle of bowl and stir. Add enough milk until the batter is fairly thick. Beat well. Have griddle hot and well oiled (not margarine, use cooking oil), but not too much oil as uneven browning may result. Drop a spoonful of the stiff batter onto the griddle (use a tablespoon). Turn once only.

Serve on hot plate. Offer a variety of jellies, butter, jam, honey and whipped cream for toppings. In America, of course, one would naturally use maple syrup. This syrup is not widely available in Australia because the climate is not conducive to maple trees—not enough rain, and too warm a climate. These days, though, imitation maple syrup is widely available. Australians do not eat pancakes for breakfast, as do Americans, and the idea that one might eat these along with syrup *and* bacon or sausage would cause any Aussie to turn up his or her nose! This is indeed strange, when one considers that Aussies eat a lot of their main meat dishes with pineapple and other sweet fruits.

11

Icings, Fillings and Spreads

Australian icing has a different consistency from the frosting most commonly found on American cakes and cookies. It is not as soft, and develops a slightly hard surface when it dries. The closest I have found to it in America is the vanilla frosting on donuts that have sat around on the shelf for most of the day. There is a type of icing used on decorative cakes, such as wedding cakes, which Australians call "plastic icing." This icing is very thick and sweet, often flavored with almond essence. As its name implies, it isn't really meant to be eaten, only for decoration.

There are many sauces, but none that one could claim are special to Australia. Lemon spreads and fillings are popular, along with various sauces that are used on Christmas puddings. Brandy cream is one such sauce.

BRANDY CREAM

| 1 | egg | $\frac{3}{4}$ | cup sugar |
| $\frac{1}{2}$-1 | cup whipped cream | 3 | tablespoons brandy |

Beat white of egg until stiff; gradually add fine sugar. Beat egg yolk slightly and add whipped cream. Fold into egg and sugar mixture. For thicker sauce, add more whipped cream. Pour in brandy slowly. When plum pudding is served piping hot, pour sauce over each serving.

ICING (FROSTING)

BOILED ICING

1	cup sugar	1	white of egg
½	cup water	1-2	drops vanilla, if required

Boil water and sugar together until a thread forms from a fork dipped into the mixture. Beat the white of egg until stiff. Allow mixture to slightly cool, then pour over egg, add vanilla if preferred, and beat until a thick cream forms. Spread over cake.

CHOCOLATE ICING

½	cup confectioners sugar	4	tablespoons grated
3	tablespoons water		chocolate *or*
		2	tablespoons cocoa

Sift sugar and place in saucepan with chocolate or cocoa. Add water and stir until warm. Spread over cake.

LEMON ICING

1 cup confectioners sugar   1 lemon

Place sugar and juice of the lemon in saucepan. Stir until all lumps are gone and a thick cream has formed. Spread over cake.

PASSION FRUIT SPREAD

Passion fruits are extremely popular in Australia, whether used in spreads, jellies or in Pavlova (see *Pavlova*, page 111) fillings. I have never found them in America, although they would thrive in a Californian climate. Passion fruit grow on a vine, which may be cultivated similar to a grape vine (although the leaves and stems are very different from grape vines). The fruit is about the size and shape of an egg, with a smooth skin, a deep brownish purple in color. When thoroughly ripe, the skin shrivels and becomes very wrinkled. This is a sign that the inside is sweet and delicious. The fruit inside is a bright yellow pulp containing scores of small black seeds.

Australians eat the seeds as well as the pulp, even though *The Joy of Cooking* recommends against it. I remember the home made vanilla ice cream my mother would make, then cut open a passion fruit and simply pour the pulp on top. But for a real treat, when we became bored with the usual run of sandwich fillings for our school lunches, she would prepare sandwiches with passion fruit spread.

3	eggs	2	ounces butter
8	passion fruits	2	cups sugar
8	tablespoons lemon juice	8	tablespoons water

Beat eggs, add rest of ingredients and mix together. Simmer until thick. Allow to cool, store in refrigerator in closed container. Spread *thinly* (see *sandwiches*, page 19) on bread and butter.

I have never seen fresh passion fruit in any American shops, or anywhere else in the Northern Hemisphere, including Italy where the climate would be ideal for their cultivation. Australia has four indigenous types of passion fruit but the one that is edible was imported from South America. I have, on occasion, found cans of passion fruit pulp (available widely in Australia) in our local gourmet food store. These are invariably excellent, even as good as the fresh pulp.

BETSY'S LEMON FILLING

1 cup sugar	1 cup water
2 lemons for juice	1-2 teaspoons grated
2 tablespoons corn flour	lemon rind
2 tablespoons custard	1 tablespoon butter
powder†	

†See page 87 about custard powder. Boil sugar, water, juice and rind together. Thicken with corn flour and custard powder, adding butter when thickened. Will set when cool.

LEMON BUTTER

1 cup sugar	2 eggs
2 ounces butter	1 lemon

Grate rind from lemon, extract juice. Soften butter, mix with sugar and rind, adding lemon juice until desired consistency.

LEMON HONEY

1 cup sugar	2 ounces butter
2 eggs	2 lemons

Grate rind from lemons, extract juice. Place all ingredients into pan and heat until thickens.

12

Drinks and Drinking

A|ustralia is a society of drinkers, of which there are two classes: tea drinkers and beer drinkers. People may be one or the other, or both, depending on the time of the day and the day of the week. The day is divided according to when one drinks, and what one drinks. Cups of tea help break up the day's work. Glasses of beer help one relax after a day's work, and pass the time on Saturdays. No beer on Sundays though. All the pubs are shut. You have to take home your bottles of beer the night before. Anyway, Sundays are more for visiting friends and relatives and drinking tea.

There are certain unwritten rules about how to fix drinks (both beer and tea) and how to behave socially when drinking. Drinking beer before lunch time on a weekday or before about 11.00 a.m. on a Saturday is considered to be a sign of an "alky" (alcoholic). The exception to this rule is when you are on a weekend binge with the mates (perhaps a footy or fishing trip) during which time it might be a sign of drinking strength to have a beer for breakfast. Tea can be taken at any hour.

Beer and tea are enjoyed especially at spectator sports, such as Aussie rules football (footy) and cricket. Actually, cricket would be dead without either. One game of cricket takes five days to finish (though it could be less). And it's probably the most boring game in the world (after baseball), whose highlights are the breaks for tea every afternoon, and the strange names for field positions (such as "silly mid on," "slips" and "square leg"). No wonder the spectators take to playing cards and drinking large quantities of beer to fill in the time between each moment of excitement when a batsman is bowled out.

The situation with footy is a little different. This game, played in the Australian winter in the Southern States (the coldest it gets is in the low 40s) is very exciting. It is played on a huge oval shaped field, about twice the size of an American football field, with 18 players on each side. Many spectators take along their flask of tea to sip and keep them warm. Few stadiums provide seating to any extent. Spectators stand for the entire game, just as they stand in the bars afterwards. Beer helps lubricate the voices of the barrackers (spectators who yell), many of whom spend much time heaping abuse on the umpire (referee). When there is a lot of beer, blues (brawls) break out among the yahoos (rowdy hooligans) and drongoes ("bloody no-hopers").

Soda is just as popular as in America. But if you ask for a soda in a milk bar (see below), you will not be understood, or will be given soda water, and thought to be weird. You have to ask for "soft drink," or ask for a specific flavor. There is a wider range of soda flavors available in Australia compared with the United States, including some hardly known here, such as passion fruit.

Aussie kids drink a lot of "cordial" which is a sweet, noncarbonated drink that is mixed up from a concentrate and tastes something like *Gatorade*. Flavors available are usually various citrus and tropical fruits.

Also popular is a powder called, variously, "lemon saline" which most Mums keep in their kitchens. This tastes not unlike some popular brands of digestive carbonating ("fizzy") drinks, such as *Brioschi*, but with a stronger lemon flavor. Saline is thought to be a very good thirst quencher.

Two other "cordials" (these are not alcoholic and are nothing like American cordials, which are called liqueurs in Australia), are worthy of mention. These are lemon squash and lime juice cordial. I have occasionally seen these in our local gourmet store, and even in our local supermarket. A little lime juice cordial mixed with cold soda water is a wonderful thirst quencher on a hot day, of which Australia has many. Lemon squash cordial is mixed with soda water to make a drink called lemon squash. One buys these mainly in a bar. They are almost acceptable in lieu of drinking beer (almost).

Many countries have distinctive settings where people traditionally meet to drink a little and talk. Australia has two such abodes. A Pub is the most widely established place to go if you wish to speak with "the locals" and drink beer. If you want to drink anything else, you are probably better off not going to a bar. I am constantly amazed at the number of pubs in every Australian town. There is certainly no shortage of them. Pubs are essentially meeting places to talk, joke, sometimes play darts or snooker, but certainly never for business. (You might be able to place a few bets as well.)

Another Australian institution is the Milk Bar. These little corner stores are everywhere in the suburbs and towns. If you like milk drinks, especially milk shakes, then these are the places to go. You will have to stand up, though, while you drink your milk shake. Milk Bars tend to be very small, and have no space for seating. Kids go to them mostly, usually on errands for Mum to buy a few small cooking items like butter or sugar; or to buy some lollies (candy) with small change.

In contrast to beer drinking, tea drinking has not until very recently taken place in public places. Tea rooms are in ample supply in England (as are Pubs), where one can get a good cup of tea, and a scone or biscuits. There have never been as many tea rooms in Australia as in England, and many of those that existed have become coffee shops that boast cappuccino and espresso coffee. But that is another story, and another cookbook! My guess is that the tea room did not flourish in Australia for the simple reason that people of my parents' generation did not trust others to make a good cup of tea. Tea was a drink made only at home. Only there could one be sure that it would be made according to one's taste. So, how to make a good cuppa?

CUPPA TEA
(CUP OF TEA)

Items and ingredients required are:
Medium Sized Teapot (preferably china)
sugar (to taste)
English breakfast tea
boiling water
tea cups and saucers
teaspoons
whole milk (to taste)
tea strainer (optional)

1. Boil water using any method. Pour a little boiling water into tea pot and swirl around so that the tea pot becomes warm. This is very important (not sure why, but it is).

2. Measure out the amount of tea you will need. One level teaspoon per cup is the usual guide, then add "one for the pot."

3. Immediately pour the rapidly boiling water into the tea pot. Replace lid, cover with a tea cosy to keep it warm. Do not place tea pot over heat, or bring to boil. This will ruin the taste of the tea (makes it taste like dish water).

4. The tea must now be left to draw for awhile. This will normally take about 5 minutes or more. Some hasten this process by lifting the tea pot and gently tilting it back and forth. It's better simply to wait. There are other things to do, anyway.

5. While the tea is drawing, ask your tea drinkers how they take their tea. In Australia, to respond that you will have yours black with lemon, while tolerated, would not be considered well. Only on special occasions do Aussies drink their tea with lemon. People do drink tea black, but most drink it white.

6. Now we come to the sticky part. It is rumored that the Queen (of England, that is) adds the milk to her tea last. The established practice in Australia is the opposite. The milk

must be placed in the cup first. The tea tastes much better this way, although you have to be more adept at guessing the amount of milk to pour in a cup, especially as you can rarely be sure how strong the tea will be when it is poured. A rule of thumb is to pour about half an inch of milk in the cup. While it is best if you didn't, it's O.K. to ask a guest whether the tea is strong enough, and to add either tea or milk to make up the desired strength.

7. Having resolved this problem to your satisfaction, place the strainer on the cup and pour the tea through it. Always pour the tea in the kitchen, then take the cup to your guest. *Never* allow any tea to splash into the saucer. (This seems a bit silly to me, since I would have thought that was exactly what the saucer was for). An alternative method is to pass around the cups, then bring the tea pot and small pitcher of milk around, and allow guests to pour their own.

8. Depending on how strong the tea pours, fill the cup to about $\frac{5}{8}$ inch from the top. If the tea strength seems alright (it should be a soft tan color), top the cup up to about $\frac{1}{8}$ inch from the top with boiling water.

9. Tea drinkers always add their own sugar if they wish.

10. A tea strainer is certainly desirable, because it makes drinking the last half inch of the tea from the cup much easier. However, there is no special rule about this. If you do not use a strainer, and your guest takes a second cup of tea, *always* empty out the dregs of tea leaves first, before refilling.

11. After you have poured the first cups of tea, refill the tea pot with more boiling water, and allow to draw once again, while you drink your first cups.

DON'T use fancy teas, rose tea, mint tea, Chinese tea, or whatever. They may be fine for other purposes, but for making a true blue Aussie cuppa, there's no place for them here.

BEER
(AND BEER DRINKING)

Making "home brew" is as popular in Australia as it is in England and America. The recipes are much the same, so I will not reproduce them here. However, with a little knowledge of the drinking customs of Aussies, one may approximate certain beer-related drinks using ingredients available in the United States.

BEER AND STOUT

Australian beers, and beers from just about everywhere can be bought from most American beverage stores these days. *Fosters* is the most widely distributed Australian beer in America. One can find those huge cans of *Fosters* and regular sized bottles in most places. *Coopers* beer (from South Australia) is also available from time to time. This beer is the closest one can get to a commercialized home brew. It has a sediment in the bottom (it's supposed to), so you need to leave the bottle sit for a day or so before you drink it. And when you pour, pour slowly so that air does not bubble back into the bottle and disturb the sediment. Leave about the last $\frac{1}{4}$ inch of sediment in the bottle. This beer is truly delicious to the beer connoisseur.

I have not seen any Australian stout (*Coopers* makes some that looks like soup) in American stores. However, the classic Irish stout, *Guinness* is available everywhere.

While stout and beer are great on their own, one can make popular Australian drinks by mixing them.

MOTHER-IN-LAW

In a 7 ounce glass, pour stout up to within $1\frac{1}{2}$ inches of the rim. Top up with a bitter beer, that is, not an ale or lager, but a beer. (Canada makes lots of these.) The name? The drink is "stout and bloody bitter."

HALF-AND-HALF

The same as for mother-in-law, but half stout and half bitter.

SHANDY

If you ask for a lemonade in Australia, you will be given a soda that looks and tastes very much like *Seven Up*. A Shandy is made by pouring beer to within $\frac{1}{2}$ inch of the top of the glass, then topping up with lemonade. Children are commonly allowed to drink a light shandy (lemonade with a dash of beer) on special occasions. Try it. Some like it, some hate it.

BEER GLASSES

Depending on which state you are in, the names of beer glasses may vary, according to shape and size. In Victoria, one may buy a "glass of beer" which is a regulation 7 ounce glass. These glasses used to be tapered from top to bottom, with a heavy base. Many different shapes have now appeared. A larger sized 10 ounce glass called a "pot" is available for those who would like to be thought of as big drinkers. If you can stand the "rubbishing" (kidding, jokes made about your personal adequacy) from your mates, you might ask for a "pony" which is a small 5 ounce glass.

By the way, Aussies have quite a disarming sense of humor, which can catch Americans unawares. The favorite pastime is to kid or rubbish mates (not usually done to strangers, unless there's good reason for it). This can amount to quite personal remarks about how one does just about everything (or how one can't do things), and appears to the outsider as insulting and uncouth. The extent to which one can take this good-natured ribbing shows how good a "bloke" (genuine fellow) one is.

In a bar, Australians will also spin yarns (tell tall tales), especially to unsuspecting visitors from another country. Again, this is part of the Aussie sense of humor, and should not be taken personally. Aussies are great kidders!

In other parts of Australia, the names of beer glasses may be different again. For example, in New South Wales, the usual sized glass is called a "middie" (10 ounces) and the larger sized is called a "schooner."

I relate all of this because Aussies take their beer drinking very seriously, as they do their tea drinking. It must be poured just right, and in the right glass. There was an outcry some years back when health regulations were introduced requiring that fresh clean glasses be provided each time the customer in a bar ordered a beer. This regulation cut across the time honored and much studied practice of always using the same glass for a refill.

The reason for this is that an experienced beer drinker can tell one glass from another, even though to the unitiated they may look the same. A fresh glass usually does not retain the head (white froth at the top) as well as a used glass. This is extremely important for Aussie beer drinkers. If you pour them a glass of beer that has no head, it will be returned to you with a comment like, "I don't drink dog's ..." Or, "What do yer think I am, a bloody Pom (Englishman)?"

It takes practice to pour a glass of beer with just the right amount of head (froth). In Victoria, a quarter of an inch of froth is considered right. The opposite is also unacceptable— too much froth. If you serve a beer with a lot of froth, an Aussie might remark, "Well, yer gonna put a bow-tie on it, mate?" An Australian will also have experimented with different detergents, to find out which ones produce the best beer glasses. Many wash their beer glasses separately from other dishes without any detergent at all, because it is thought that detergent ruins the head keeping capabilities of the glass. Many hours may be passed in a bar discussing the science of beer pouring.

DRINKING BEER—AUSSIE STYLE

Unless you visit Australia, you will not have to be concerned with some of the hints provided in this section. But it might be fun to have an Aussie night with your friends, if you have any who like beer drinking.

The most important thing to know is how to behave in an Aussie bar. Here are a few hints.

1. If you are female, it's probably best not to go into a public bar in an Aussie Pub. There's no law against it (though there used to be!), but not many do. You would be best advised to find the "Ladies Lounge" or "Saloon Bar" where the

surroundings and clientele would be more designed for sheilas (girls).

2. To soften the shock of entering into a Public Bar, try the Saloon Bar first. This is a special part of the bar set aside for those who are prepared to pay a little more for their glass of beer, and enjoy slightly better, and quieter surroundings. It is O.K. to ask for mixed drinks in this bar, or the Ladies Lounge, where it's expected.

3. If you are taken to the bar with some new found Aussie mates, beware! I have known a number of Americans who visited Australia on business, and after the working day they were spirited off to the pub to "have a few." A great Aussie pastime is to initiate foreigners into Aussie beer drinking. The rate of drinking is usually much faster than the innocent visitor is accustomed to, and the beer tends to pack a bigger kick.

4. If you find yourself in a "drinking school" (a group of 3 or more drinkers) then you may be in trouble. Tradition requires that each member of the school "shout" (take his turn in paying for a round of drinks). Anyone who pulls out in the middle of a round, or who doesn't take his turn, is considered to be a bludger (free loader). Obviously, if the school is large, you're in for quite a time. The only way to extricate oneself from such a situation is to pay for an extra round of drinks before you leave.

5. If you are alone, be careful which stool you sit on. Very often there are set places where the local boozers (steady drinkers) always sit. Years ago, when I lived in a pub, I saw "blues" (rowdy rough brawls) caused by such inconsiderate behavior.

6. If you are careful to abide by these rules, you can go into any Aussie bar and expect to be treated well. Though they are rowdy places, smoke-filled and smelling of yeast and beer soaked into the very woodwork of the buildings, they are also congenial places, where one can always find a mate to talk to.

The tradition of heavy beer drinking probably dates back to shearing times late in the 19th century. The shearers would work constantly until the shearing was done, receiving meals and lodging on the homestead. When the shearing was com-

pleted the men would be paid their checks. Many took off to
the nearest pub in search of relaxation and excitement. To be
"lambed down" was to be led astray by others, or oneself, into
spending an entire check on booze:

> The shades of night were falling fast,
> As down a steep gully passed
> A man whom you could plainly see
> Had just come off a drunken spree,
>   Lambed down.
> He'd left the station with his check,
> And little evil did he reck;
> At Ryan's pub he felt all right,
> And yet he was, before next night,
>   Lambed down.
> 'Oh, stay! old Ryan said, 'and slip
> Your blanket off, and have a nip;
> I'll cash your check and send you on.'
> He stopped, and now his money's gone—
>   Lambed down.
> He's got the shakes and thinks he sees
> Blue devils lurking in the trees;
> Oh, shearers! if you've any sense
> Don't be on such pretence
>   Lambed down.

—*Lambed Down*, Anonymous, about 1870.

13

Outback Cooking

$\boxed{\text{A}}$merica has her Wild West. Australia has her Outback. Many of Australia's most moving novels are set in the Outback. There lies the mystery and romance of Australia. The outback is enormous, about four fifths of the country's area. There is also a lot of bush land, less desolate, populated by more wild life, in high plains surrounding the coastal areas where there is a little more rain. Of course, in the North East, where the climate is tropical, there is abundant wild life.

The scarcity of water shapes much of Australia's landscape. There is the constant fear of bushfires which occur every summer, and wreak terrible destruction. Yet many of the eucalyptus forests require the heat of fire to break open their nuts (gum nuts) so that they may germinate and renew the forest.

I have included a chapter on Outback cooking because there are a few classic dishes and methods of cooking that are fun to do, some of which one can reproduce in the American forest. In fact, there is greater opportunity to try out bush cooking in many parts of the United States because the danger of forest fires is not so great (depending, of course, on where one lives in the States).

If you do try some Outback cooking, please, please use fire safety. Don't have a large fire, just a very small one is needed for most cooking, and clear the ground for 10 feet around. Preferably, use the safest type of cooking fire, a trench fire. All one needs is a small trench dug in the ground, with the fire lit in the trench. In most of Australia during the summer

months, it would be extremely unlikely that one could light a
cooking fire in the bush, due to the danger of fire (and there are
severe punishments for doing so). Most Aussies, during these
months, if they do want to cook outdoors, will use a portable
gas barbecue. But there are even many days of extreme fire
danger when gas barbecues cannot be used.

The best time to cook in the Australian bush is in the late
winter or early spring. The smell of eucalyptus just after it
has rained is hard to beat. Better, I think, than the smell of a
pine forest, though this is a little bit like comparing rubies and
diamonds. By the way, Australians call eucalyptus trees "gum
trees." There are about 1,000 varieties, of which the famed
koala eats only one.

About killing and eating Australian wild life. Killing animals in order to eat, if one is actually dependent on the land
for survival, seems reasonable to me. But I doubt that there
is anyone who actually does this in Australia today, including
the Australian Aborigines. I have included some recipes that
require that you have in hand a dead animal or two. Frankly,
they're included for the sake of curiosity. I wouldn't want to
see a single hair (or scale) of any Australian animal harmed.
And I'm sure just about every Australian thinks the same way,
in spite of what you may have seen on American television.

BUSH ANGELS

If you just happen to be trudging through the bush, and just happen to have brought along the following ingredients, you could make these outback desserts and late night snacks when you're telling yarns around the campfire.

slices of bread
can of condensed milk
shredded coconut

In order to make this delicacy, you will need at least 1 grubby (i.e. sticky and dirty) child. Have this chosen kid dip the bread in the sticky condensed milk, a part of bush cooking that only kids could enjoy. Now, cross your fingers, and hope that the bread is not dropped on the bush floor (always dry and dusty). Have your child press the milk-soaked bread in the coconut. Toast over hot coals. Insist that the child hand over the first cooked Bush angel to you (if it's clean). These are only for sugar-holics, which means that if you were thinking of sneaking a quick beer before going to bed, forget it.

Make sure the billy is boiling, and you can sip down a cup of delicious billy tea as you munch on your Angels. How much closer to Heaven could you get? If you take a moment to forget your sticky fingers, you may look up at the huge expanse of the Southern Hemisphere (looks bigger than the Northern Sky). The sky is always clear, the stars twinkle without fail every night. The Southern Cross is there. Find an Aussie mate to point it out for you.

KANGAROO TAIL SOUP

1	kangaroo tail	$2\frac{1}{2}$	pints water
	(about 3 pound)	1	onion
1	carrot	$\frac{1}{2}$	turnip or small
1	stick celery		rutabagas
3	ounces barley	1	teaspoon chopped parsley
	salt and pepper		

Wash the tail, trim off fat, divide at joints. Remove meat from bones and cut into small pieces. In a large pan, place bones, meat, salt and pepper, and barley and bring slowly to the boil. Skim off fat just before and after boiling.

Prepare vegetables, dicing small. Add to the soup after it boils and simmer for $2\frac{1}{2}$ hours. Remove bones, add additional salt and pepper to taste. Skim off fat if necessary, add parsley. Serve with crisp croutons. Aussies will take it with hot buttered toast.

Please don't visit Australia with the hope of shooting a kangaroo, not to mention eating it! It is true that in certain parts of Australia, the Northern arid areas, kangaroos are thought of as pests by some farmers. This is because they compete with farmers' cattle and sheep for that great scarcity in the Australian Outback: life-sustaining grass. Kangaroos are especially a nuisance because they tend to eat the grass down and into the roots, thus destroying the plant, making it difficult to regenerate. In these areas, so I am told, kangaroos are not a protected species, although particular species (such as the Big Red) are protected and endangered.

In my home town there are many kangaroos in the surrounding bush. They come down to feed on the golf course, which is a convenient source of rich green grass. It is sometimes necessary to shoo them out of the way so one can tee off or putt. While they are tame enough, they will not let one touch them, which is probably pretty smart. I have often wondered whether they laughed at my swing, as they watched nonchalantly chewing their breakfast.

ROAST RABBIT

1	rabbit	3	slices bacon
4	tablespoons flour		salt and pepper
	stuffing		

STUFFING

$\frac{1}{2}$	cup breadcrumbs	1	tablespoon chopped parsley
	grated lemon rind	$\frac{1}{2}$	teaspoon salt
$\frac{1}{4}$	teaspoon pepper		pinch nutmeg
1	teaspoon butter	$\frac{1}{4}$	cup milk

Soak and wash rabbit, as per instructions page 71. Make stuffing, insert in rabbit and sew up. Rub with seasoned flour, lay bacon slices on top. Fatty bacon is better in this case, as rabbit flesh is very lean. Place in baking pan with vegetable oil, cover lightly with aluminum foil, and bake $1\frac{1}{2}$ to 2 hours at 400^0. Baste every 15 minutes. Australians do not, as a rule, use cranberry sauce, as the climate is not conducive to the growth of cranberries (not enough water and not cold enough). However, cranberry sauce would be an excellent accompaniment to roast rabbit. Some Australian recipes recommend red or black currant jelly.

Rabbits are not indigenous to Australia, so I guess they are fair game. If you are stuck in the bush without any food (Heaven knows how you would get into such a predicament), a rabbit might just save your skin. They're difficult to catch, though, unless you can use some of the (cruel) methods I described on page 70. If you're lucky, they can also be easy. I was once walking in the bush with my father, who pointed out the knee-high tufts of thick grass. These were, he said, favorite sitting spots for rabbits. Suddenly he stopped, and put his finger to his mouth. He was poised over a big tuft of grass. He gave a loud clap, and a rabbit flew out from under us at lightening speed. This rabbit was duly caught and eaten.

I prefer chicken, myself.

ROAST QUAIL

quail
1 slice of bacon per quail
vine leaves
1 ounce melted butter
fried bread
red currant jelly
dried breadcrumbs

To clean and pluck quail, see below. Truss quail and brush with melted butter. Place a vine leaf on the breast and on top of this, a bacon slice. Secure with a strong tooth pick or skewer. Cover lightly with aluminum foil and roast $\frac{1}{2}$ hour at 400⁰. Baste frequently. To fry bread, heat oil to very hot, as for French fries, drop in squares of day old bread. Quickly brown and remove, so that it remains crisp. Serve quail on fried bread, spread with red currant jelly. Top with gravy sprinkled with dried breadcrumbs.

Quail are found in most parts of Australia where they nest in long dry grass. They are a tiny fat bird (a relative of the grouse, I'm told). Their flocking together when disturbed is remarkable.

To prepare quail: Do not scald bird, as the skin will break. Pluck feathers from one side, holding bird by leg, then by wing. If feathers are difficult to remove, pour boiling water over difficult part. Cut head off, place bird on breast and cut slit in back of neck, pull neck out and cut off close to the body. Cut between vent and tail, pull out entrails with fingers. Chop off legs above the knee joint. Rinse out inside of bird.

I know you'll probably never shoot your own quail, but I've included this just to add a little genuine Outback flavor. This recipe would go very nicely substituting the small cornish hens one finds in the supermarket.

JUGGED HARE

You need a large "jug" or jar in order to prepare this unusual dish. One is not likely to have such an implement in the Outback. But you never know, you may just happen on a lonely homestead a couple of days after you catch the hare.

1 young hare
$\frac{1}{2}$ inch slice of bacon
3 sprigs of thyme
1 onion
pepper and salt
$\frac{3}{4}$ cup flour

Skin and clean the hare, and hang it head down for 2 days (1 day if it's too bloody hot to sit out in the sun). It would be best to do something to keep the blowies (flies) away from it while hanging. Take a large wide-mouthed stoneware jar. Place hare in jar, cut bacon into small cubes. Add bacon, onion, thyme, salt and pepper. Make a smooth paste with flour and add to hare. Add more water until hare is just covered. Cover jar with cloth or aluminum (called al-u-min-ium by Aussies) foil, and place in a saucepan of hot water. Boil for 3 to 4 hours, depending on size and age of hare.

To skin a hare or rabbit: Using a very sharp knife, cut around the neck, and make a small incision under tail. Open hare's mouth as wide as possible, and force fist down gullet, keeping two fingers pushed out front. Retract and extend fingers once or twice to loosen insides. Push hand further into hare's gullet until index finger reaches tail. Force finger through small incision and curl around tail. Pull tail through incision and grip in hand. With other hand, push down strongly on head of rabbit. With a strong flicking movement across the knee, pull hare inside out. Remove entrails. Reverse procedure, then peel off skin beginning around neck, and pulling down to tail.

DAMPER

flour
water
butter
jellies and jams
honey
salt
a green stick

Damper is a traditional scone-like bread baked over or on the camp fire. The trick is as much in the cooking as it is in the mixing.

1. Prepare a cooking fire by allowing a reasonably large fire to burn down to a heap of red coals.

2. Select a green stick, about 3 feet long, that is straight and about $\frac{1}{2}$ inch thick. Try to get one that doesn't require chopping down a whole tree.

3. Place flour and salt in mixing bowl, add water a little at a time until a thick dough is formed. Keep the dough as stiff as possible. Knead well and allow to sit for an hour or so. Roll into a long sausage shape, then twist around the green stick so it resembles the doctor's emblem of a serpent on a staff.

5. Place stick with damper over fire. The easiest way to cook this damper is to rest the stick on one or two forked sticks, so you don't have to hold it all the time. Turn the damper over every now and again. The most important thing to watch is not to cook the damper too quickly. It may take an hour or more.

6. When cooked, remove from fire and break damper from stick. Serve pieces smothered with butter, jam, jellies or honey. Though it's not Australian, try some maple syrup as well.

VARIATIONS: Knead into a ball and place at side of fire, and allow to cook slowly in the embers. If the fire is slow enough, you can leave the damper to cook for 1 to 2 hours. Enclose an egg inside the dough. It will be nicely cooked when you retrieve the damper.

BILLY TEA

Many of the rules of tea making described on page 132 apply to making billy tea. However there are a few differences.

First, you must have a "billy." This is a large can-like metal container, with a wire handle attached to the top. This is not very functional because when the billy is boiling, it's very hard to pick up—the wire handle hangs down close to the fire, and against the hot side of the billy. It takes a little practice to thread a strong stick, or your hunting knife under the handle so you can lift the billy off without burning your fingers.

1. Prepare a hot, but small fire. Place the billy $\frac{3}{4}$ full of water on the flames. A black soot coated billy is better, as it heats more quickly. (How you carry it with your other things without getting black all over you is your problem).

2. When the water is boiling, remove the billy from the fire as quickly as possible, and *immediately* add about 6 teaspoons of tea (English Breakfast Tea—nothing fancy), depending on the size of the billy. Usually, allow 1 teaspoon for each cup of tea to be made.

3. Do not return the billy to the fire. Leave to the side to keep hot, but do not allow to boil. If the tea boils it will taste like bitter soup.

4. Now is the time for the tea to "draw." It is best left to sit for a few minutes. There are various beliefs about how the drawing process may be speeded up. Some advise taking the billy by the handle and swinging it forcefully and evenly round and round over one's head. I have seen this done, and it does seem to work. However, I have also seen the billy fly away from the handle several times. A gentler way is to tap all around the sides of the billy with a teaspoon.

5. Pour tea as reported in *cuppa tea*, page 132. Milk should be added first. When drinking tea in the Outback, one never drinks from a cup and saucer. An enamel mug is the traditional container, though not my choice, because it conducts the heat so fiercely that one can burn one's lips very easily.

BUSH VARIATION: Some hardy Outback types claim to
drink billy tea flavored with a gum leaf (leaf from a eucalyptus
tree). If you decide to try this, choose a sweet smelling tree,
and break only a tiny piece of leaf ($\frac{1}{4}$ inch at the most) into
the tea while it is drawing. It is best to drink eucalyptus tea
without milk.

It is widely believed that eucalyptus trees have medicinal
value. Eucalyptus oil is sold everywhere in Australia for the
treatment of cold symptoms. When I was camping in the Outback many years ago, one of our party had a bad cold. He
decided to sleep on a bed of fresh eucalyptus leaves. He lay
back in bliss, and inhaled the beautiful healing fumes. When
we awoke in the morning, we beheld our friend burned all over
the color of a lobster. The fumes had been far too strong. And
he still had his cold.

The Australian's love of billy tea is expressed in this bush
ballad:

> You may talk of your whisky or talk of your beer,
> I've something far better awaiting me here;
> It stands on that fire beneath the gum tree,
> And you cannot much †lick it—a billy of tea.
> So fill up your tumbler as high as you can,
> You'll never persuade me it's not the best plan,
> To let all the beer and spirits go free
> And stick to my darling old billy of tea.
> And at night when I camp, if the day has been
>   warm,
> I give each of the horses their ‡tucker of corn,
> Then the fire I start and the water I get,
> And the corned beef and damper in order I set,
> But I don't touch the ‡grub, though so hungry I
>   be,
> I wait till it's ready—the Billy of Tea.

—*The Billy of Tea*, Anonymous, about 1840.

   † *To lick* someone or something is to win or do better than.
It does not mean to give a beating as in American usage.

   ‡ *Grub* and *tucker* mean food.

EGGS 'N ORANGES

This recipe will not work with Emu eggs. You need chook eggs (page 55).

hen eggs
large oranges
salt and pepper

With a sharp knife, cut out the top of each orange, making an opening big enough for an egg. Scoop out the flesh then insert the egg.

Prepare a slow fire with plenty of glowing coals. Make small holes in the coals and place the oranges with eggs in the coals. The heat of the fire along with the juice still left in the orange skin, will actually boil your egg. Depending on how hot your fire is, remove egg in orange when cooked (usually about 7 minutes).

This is a great way to get kids to cook eggs. I can't guarantee they'll eat them though.

VARIATIONS: Many quick cooking foods may be prepared in this way. (1) If you would rather avoid the orange flavor, find a flat rock with a depression, not too hard to find in a creek bed. Clean it off, place over a very hot fire, and when hot, break your egg into the natural pan made by the depression in the rock. The egg will cook right before your eyes. Or, cut hole in slice of bread, lay on hot flat rock, break egg into hole. Of course, the standard practice of enclosing the food in wet clay then placing this on the fire is also an effective way to cook. Depending on the clay, though, you might need a hammer to break it open once it has baked. (2) Attach a green vine or wet string to a safety pin, stick pin through shell of egg, and suspend egg over fire until cooked. Sounds crazy, but it works! (3) Encase food in banana skins and cook the same as in oranges. (4) For dessert, core apples, fill with raisins and sugar. If they will fit in orange cases, cook as above, otherwise, coat with clay and cook.

FRIED TIGER SNAKE

Tiger snake
herbs, preferably chives
salt and pepper
cooking oil

Tiger snakes, one of the most poisonous snakes in the world, are only found in Australia. They are named because of their distinctive yellow and brown stripes. They are not large snakes, as snakes go. The largest I have seen in the bush was about 3 feet. Most are about 2 feet or less, and the thickness of a hot dog. If you are bitten by one, you've probably had it, unless you can get to a hospital for an antidote right away. I strongly recommend that you do not go hunting for one of these nasties, just so you can try out this recipe (though I would be flattered).

In case you are foolish enough to track one down, here's how to do it. Actually, Tiger snakes are rather timid, and will not attack you unless you happen accidentally to stand on them. If you make a lot of noise walking through long dry grass in summer in a field populated by Tiger Snakes, you can see the grass swirling, and hear the swishing as the snakes speed away from you.

The way to catch one is to leave food, especially sugar, around your camp. This is no surprise, is it? It's the same way you can catch a bear (or for it to catch you!) in North American forests. This is how I had my first (and only) encounter with two Tiger snakes, an adult of about 3 feet, and a baby of about 1 foot. They got into our tucker box (food box).

Old hands claim that the best way to kill a Tiger snake is to use a pliable long wire that will, with a strong flick of the arm, crack down on the snake's back and break it. I tried this, and couldn't get it to work. By far the most effective way is to use a long forked stick to push down on the snake, pinning it to the ground just behind the head. If you are an experienced bushman, you will be wearing strong boots, and with the heel of such boot, bring it down on the head and crush it. It helps to have a mate do this, or hold the stick down for you.

If you follow these directions you will have yourself a dead snake—at least that's what I think. It is believed that the Tiger snake, no matter what you do to it, never dies until sundown.

To prepare Tiger Snake: With a sharp knife, and the snake definitely dead, cut off the head. Draw the knife down the belly from tip to toe (so to speak). Dip the snake into boiling water, then work the point of the knife under the skin at the neck, and loosed skin all around. Roll back skin, have a mate hold body of snake at neck, peel skin completely off. Remove entrails (not much to remove) or leave and discard after cooking. Cut into sections.

Heat oil in old bush frying pan until quite hot. Quickly fry snake until golden brown. Serve sprinkled with chopped chives or parsley. If you can find some wild asparagus (sometimes found along the edges of irrigation canals) boil and serve also. Salt and pepper a must. Vegetables are important with this dish. Potatoes (regular, not yams) baked in the fire's coals go nicely with this dish. Do not over cook, or meat will be tough. (It's tough anyway, but then, what can you expect?) Frankly, even though they are poisonous, I'd rather Tiger snakes weren't killed. They're part of Australia, after all.

WITCHETY GRUBS

Witchety grubs (from the Aboriginal *witjute*, the name of roots in which the grubs are often found) are various larvae that feed in the wood of eucalytptus trees, most often between the bark and the trunk. They are about 1 to $2\frac{1}{2}$ inches long, with a fat creamy body about the width of a man's thumb, and stumpy legs. The Australian Aborigines who live in the Outback are said to consider them a delicacy. As with most food taken by the Aborigines in the Outback, they eat their witchety grubs raw. I have never tried them prepared in that way. I recommend them cooked as follows, Outback style.

> witchety grubs
> an old piece of metal
> salt and pepper to taste
> a little cooking oil (optional)
> yams†

So you're stuck in the Outback without anything except a little salt and pepper! The Outback is desolate often without vegetation, but one is sure to find somewhere a scrap piece of metal left from some failed effort to drive an enormous distance, or maybe from a *Mad Max* movie set.

Scrub the metal clean, hopefully in a little sand and water from a nearby trickling creek. Prepare a fast, trench fire and place the metal across the top. Immediately place yams in coals beside the fire. After about $\frac{1}{2}$ an hour, when the hot plate is quite hot, drop the witchety grubs down and rapidly roll across the metal plate. Keep rolling until they are browned all over. Remove from heat, allow to cool. Remove yams from coals. Break open yams and serve each yam with a witchety grub nestled in the middle.

Next page please...

On a dare, I once ate a witchety grub cooked according to this recipe. It tasted quite delicious, somewhere between roast pork and chicken, and it stayed down too. But I have to admit that I haven't eaten one since.

Grub is a word used by Australians to refer to any larvae found in the garden and elsewhere. When I have asked my American friends what a grub is, they invariably reply that it is a "freeloader" and rarely relate the word to insects (real insects that is). Australians have their own word for a freeloader: a *bludger*.

BAKED EEL

Although Australia has a dry climate, there are many small rivers and creeks that run in winter and spring. They are teaming with freshwater eels, as well as other freshwater fish. I include eels, and not other fish, because eels are the easiest to catch (that is to say, they are the only darned fish I ever managed to catch). As for fishermen everywhere, a plentiful supply of beer is needed in order to snare these creatures, usually very late at night.

When you hook these eels, you will think you have a shark on the line. They fight to the death, often tearing their bodies off the hook in order to get free.

Prepare as for Tiger snake, page 151. Prepare fire and hot plate as for Witchety grubs, page 152, but do not have fire quite as hot. Roll pieces of eel across hot plate. Depending on type of eel and where you caught it, flesh may be quite fatty. Cook until fat has run out. Serve with baked yams.†

---

†Yams are a type of sweet potato cultivated in many parts of Australia and the South Pacific generally. If preferred, ordinary potatoes could be substituted, and cooked in the same manner.

BUNYIP BUNS

I have saved this recipe till last, abiding by the principle that I have held to since childhood: I have always kept the best till last. When a kid, I ate vegetables first, pie crusts and other tasty morsels last.

The Bunyip is a mysterious animal (far more mysterious than the Tasmanian Devil) which has been sighted only by the most experienced Outback bushmen. I can claim to have made at least one sighting, and possibly two, both late at night, during fishing trips with my mates. I have spoken to many other experienced Outback campers who have also confirmed the existence of this animal.

The Bunyip is a diurnal animal, but is so well camouflaged (it not only changes color, but also shape) that it is difficult to distinguish from the grays, browns and whites of ghost gums (a particular type of eucalyptus tree, made famous by the Aboriginal artist, Albert Namatjira). It is also a cowardly animal, and has been known to hide behind other animals when it observed the barrel of a hunter's gun.

Nothing is known of its reproductive cycle, except the one thing that makes it possible to share this recipe with you. It establishes nesting places made of a strange fibrous substance, rather similar to the truffles dug up in northern Italy. In fact, it is possible to find these bunyip nests using small piglets, properly trained. One must be very lucky to find Bunyip hollows. Although Bunyips are sighted mostly where ghost gums grow, one cannot be sure that bunyip nests will be found in the same place. Furthermore, it is claimed by some old timers that Bunyips systematically destroy their nests every few days—or at least move them to other places—in order to fool would-be nest farmers.

2	cups plain flour	$1\frac{1}{4}$	cups milk
$\frac{1}{4}$	cup sugar	2	ounces butter
1	egg	1	packet yeast
1	teaspoon salt	1	Bunyip nest

Mix yeast with a little warm milk and sugar, add rest of milk (warmed) and let stand 10 minutes. Rub butter into flour until it looks like oatmeal, then add sugar and salt.

Wash and drain Bunyip nest well, removing any pieces of fur or feathers that may be attached. Clip off any black pieces—these are old and bitter. A fresh nest will be a rich brown in color and will have a smell similar to that of fresh cut grass. Break in pieces, place in blender and grind. Add to flour mixture.

Add yeast mixture and beaten egg. Mix with wooden spoon, and work into soft dough. Knead well, then make balls of dough about half the size of tennis balls and place on greased cookie tray. Cover with damp dish cloth and leave in warm place until dough rises to about double the size. Boil a little sugar with one cinnamon stick in water, and glaze tops of buns. Bake at 420^0 for about 20 minutes, or until golden brown.

Serve hot with butter, sprinkle with sugar and cocoa, or powdered hot chocolate. Add one grain of salt.

Bunyip

Stir the Wallaby Stew

Poor Dad he got five years or more as everybody
   knows,
And now he lives in Maitland Jail with broad ar-
   rows on his clothes,
He branded all of Brown's clean-skins and never
   left a tail,
So I'll relate the family's woes since Dad got put in
   jail.
Chorus
     So stir the wallaby stew,
     Make soup of the kangaroo tail,
     I tell you things is pretty tough
     Since Dad got put in jail.
They let Dad out before his time, to give us a surprise.
He came and slowly looked around and gently blessed our eyes,
He shook hands with the shearer cove and said he
   thought things stale,
So left things here to shepherd us and battled back
   to jail.

—Anonymous, mid 1800s.

Wallaby (Small Kangaroo)

Index

Icings, Fillings and Spreads

Outback Cooking

Steak, Chops and Snags

NOTES

NOTES